A Guide to the
Northern Ireland Assembly

agreeing to disagree?

edited by Robin Wilson
with a foreword by John Mullin

The Stationery Office

The Stationery Office 2001

Applications for reproduction should be made in writing to
The Stationery Office Limited St Crispins,
Duke Street, Norwich NR3 1PD

The information contained in the publication is believed to be correct
at time of manufacture. Whilst care has been taken to ensure that the
information is accurate, the publisher can accept no responsibility for
any errors or omissions or for changes to the details given.

A cip catalogue record for this book is available from the British Library.
A Library of Congress cip catalogue record has been applied for

First published 2001

ISBN 0 11 4972575

Contents

Contributors

Richard Barnett is professor of public finance and management at the University of Ulster

Paul Bew is a professor of politics at Queen's University Belfast

Dominic Bryan lectures in the Institute of Irish Studies at Queen's University Belfast

John Coakley is a senior lecturer in politics at University College Dublin

Paul Dixon lectures in the School of Public Policy, Economics and Law at the University of Ulster

Sydney Elliott is a senior lecturer in politics at Queen's University Belfast

Tom Hadden is a professor of law at Queen's University Belfast

Colin Harvey is professor of constitutional and human rights law at the University of Leeds

Colin Knox is professor of public policy at the University of Ulster

Elizabeth Meehan is a professor of politics and Jean Monnet professor of European social policy at Queen's University Belfast

John Mullin is Deputy Editor of The Scotsman. He was the former Ireland correspondent of The Guardian

Duncan Morrow is a lecturer in politics at the University of Ulster

Henry Patterson is a professor of politics at the University of Ulster

Rick Wilford is a reader in politics at Queen's University Belfast

Robin Wilson is director of Democratic Dialogue

John Woods is regional director of Friends of the Earth in Northern Ireland

Preface

■ **D**evolution has been a UK-wide phenomenon following the election of the Labour government in 1997 (even if some English regions do not yet feel their case has been heard). Based on *A Guide to the Scottish Parliament,* published by the Stationery Office in 1999, this book sets out to provide a guide to the Northern Ireland Assembly.

But while the Northern Ireland Assembly has similar powers to those of the Scottish Parliament, its history is tortuous, its institutional and context complicated, and its future uncertain. So the book falls into three sections:

- the historical background,
- the Belfast agreement, and
- future prospects.

The collection has been assembled by a team of experts, mainly drawn from Northern Ireland's two universities and its think tank, Democratic Dialogue. I am very grateful for the generous assistance of all contributors—particularly since the vicissitudes of the implementation of the Belfast agreement have meant the project has been twice previously put on hold.

ROBIN WILSON

Foreword

John Mullin

■ It was May 1991, and I was dispatched to Heathrow Airport, with instructions to board the same flight back to Belfast as the Rev Ian. He had just gone with Jim Molyneaux, the other leader of Unionism, for talks at Downing Street. This was, strangely perhaps, something of a newsworthy event at the time, for it had been no fewer than 10 years since a PM had granted such an audience. My instructions were to accompany the Big Man back to Belfast, and file some colour. Nonsense, of course, but the usual fare of newspapers.

Anyway, it never quite worked out like that, and, five hours on, I was still sitting there as the last flight was due to leave Gate 47 at 10.15 pm. I asked the paper if I could go in any case, and, the news desk guy, a previous Northern Ireland correspondent himself, sighed long and loud, and said OK.

So it was 90 or so minutes later I sat in the back of a mini-cab, having pulled out of the airport and stopped suddenly in the middle of nowhere, talking to the back of a head and listening to this weird, vaguely terrifying accent. All sort of things were going through my head as a car soon arrived behind us, flashed its lights and pulled in. It was, rather prosaically, another taxi-driver, paying back the fiver he owed my man.

Northern Ireland is a place which suffers from the most marked misinterpretation from those who have never been there, and, incidentally, for some who do and who should know better. My mother, bless her, was always convinced I was going to end up with a bullet in my head or blown to pieces, when, of course, if you lived in a nice district you could have lived through the entire Troubles without seeing a soldier. Sort of.

My love for it was sealed on my first wander into Belfast city centre, a mini-pub crawl during which four different sets of folk asked me to join them for a chat.

It was the humour I liked. Walk into a bar in Dublin, and, sure, you can strike up a conversation. You are a racing certainty to be your new-found companion's new-found best friend. But in Belfast, they take the mickey out of our jacket, your haircut, or your accent, and they expect you to respond in kind. My type of place. I even like the way the hard men say hello, a near imperceptible flick of the head, uncompromising yet friendly.

I recall my first door-knock up the Falls Road after some poor Catholic had been killed in an IRA coffee jar bomb attack gone wrong. His neighbours were all gathered in clumps on the doorsteps, and I thought I would be in for a doing. Not a bit of it. I had the full story within five minutes, and tea and chocolate biscuits too.

For six years after that, I was sent out to Northern Ireland whenever the then Guardian's correspondent was on holiday, or there had been a particularly vicious disaster, requiring a second hand. I was there for the miseries on the Shankill Road, at Greysteel and Loughinisland, and several more killings where virtually all aside from their families will have long forgotten the details, if they ever knew them, that is.

I was night editor, a relatively esteemed position, when The

Guardian eventually asked me to go there full-time. I was 34, not long married, and a new father, and I had always thought the time best to do such a job was five years or so earlier. I had a nice life in London, and was well-set on the executive ladder. After a fashion.

I said yes, without hesitation, and arrived in September 1997. I never regretted the decision for a second.

I thought I knew the place a bit. But the funny thing was that, over the next three years, I just kept finding out more things I never knew I never knew, if you get my drift.

It was the beginning of perhaps the most astonishing phase of all in of what we euphemistically call The Troubles, with Sinn Fein just about to join the all-party talks which would lead to the Good Friday Agreement, and the IRA to split again, with the foundation of a group which was to be responsible within a year for the worst ever atrocity in Northern Ireland. So much happened: an agreement, an assembly, an executive (twice); Drumcree (thrice); Mo Mowlam, Peter Mandleson, terrible killings, and horrendous feuds.

I remember crying on the street in Omagh only four days after the car bomb there, and after almost all the funerals were finished. In contrast, I wept at Ballymoney, where three young brothers died in a terrible petrol-bombing, even as I was covering the story. A neighbour had told me how one of the boys had cried: "My feet are burning."

I know there are some people who find the issues thrown up in Northern Ireland impenetrable and even boring, and who write the people who live there off. To do so is almost a crime.

Politics in Northern Ireland are more than about systems of government. They are about people, and they are fine folk, witty, confident and, despite it all strong.

Robin Wilson, whom I had known through his work with Fortnight, the current affairs magazine before he went on to head Democratic Dialogue, the think-tank, was always a source of excellent advice to me. Through his academic rigour and, perhaps more importantly, his feel for the issues, he has resisted the common fate of many commentators, to become pigeonholed. As well as his intelligence, his objectivity was his most important asset, and I am honoured to be asked to write this, unashamedly personal, foreword.

I left Belfast two months ago, to come back to my native Scotland as deputy editor of The Scotsman. I miss Northern Ireland very much, and, while hoping this doesn't sound too over the top, I really hope everything works out there. The ordinary men and women deserve it.

Introduction: politics or polarisation?

Robin Wilson

A matter of perspective

■ **N**early three years after the Belfast Agreement, Northern Ireland remains a society ill at ease with itself. In a manner often baffling to outside observers, it continues to oscillate between political stabilisation and intercommunal polarisation (Hayes and McAllister, 1999).

At one level, the region is much more peaceful, in terms of lives needlessly lost to violence. Yet at another, sectarian intimidation, mainly of Catholics, and attacks on premises associated with either main religious group – such as Catholic churches and Orange halls – were, at the time of writing, a daily occurrence (see, for example, Irish Times, July 19th 2000). From one view, the political institutions arising from the agreement retained strong support. Yet from another perspective both Protestant alienation and Catholic assertiveness seemed to be increasing, as reflected in growing support for the Democratic Unionist Party and Sinn Féin.

For many years, the prevailing international view of Northern Ireland was that it was a quasi-colonial situation from which the only viable resolution lay in Irish unification (Guelke, 1988). But in the 1990s, particularly after the war in ex-Yugoslavia, it became increasingly evident that here was an ethno-nationalist conflict (Hayes and McAllister, 1999: 35) whose resolution depended on intercommunal accommodation.

Reaching, and then implementing and sustaining, such an agreement was by no means easy. The Balkan conflict, after all, was only 'resolved' by the expulsion of the Serb minority from Croatia, the involution of Serbia and an ethnic carve-up of Bosnia-Hercegovina – which left the Kosovo tinderbox ready to ignite. Similarly, the Oslo peace accords may have led to a handshake on the White House lawn, but the process they set in train was one of a divorce between Israelis and Palestinians, not a new co-existence. Partition had already been tried in Ireland – a hardly happy experience – and cantonisation of the intermingled northern populations would require brutal 'ethnic cleansing'. For better or worse, Protestants and Catholics would have to share the same political space, in a world where proliferating intra-state and paramilitary conflicts provide an inauspicious backdrop (Kaldor, 1999).

Moreover, the most significant actor in the equation – by virtue of the force it could threaten rather than the mandate it could secure – was the republican movement. But the Irish Republican Army and its political wing, Sinn Féin, rejected entirely the 'revisionist' analysis that Northern Ireland was a community-relations problem. And its tantalising offer of an end to its campaign of violence in return for ratchet political progress towards its united-Ireland goal encouraged governments in Dublin, the United States and (less enthusiastically) London to jolly republicans along. In the process, the Social Democratic and Labour Party, formerly dominant within the Catholic community, began to be eclipsed.

As this 'peace process' developed in the early-mid 90s, Northern

Ireland's Protestant community became increasingly restless, torn between those who sniffed 'betrayal' by Perfidious Albion to IRA 'terrorism' and those who insisted republican advances could only be stemmed by taking on SF in negotiations. This latter position, associated with the originally hard-line Ulster Unionist leader, David Trimble, was to prevail. But it was an argument about tactics, not about the politics of the Catholic community; to say it was moderate is not to say it was conciliatory.

Institutionalising the conflict

■ **T**he Belfast Agreement essentially shoehorned these mistrustful protagonists into an institutional arrangement through which they could conduct their antagonism as attrition rather than aggression. There was perhaps an unspoken hope that, as the institutions became like an old suit of clothes for the participants at Stormont, they would come to wear them with more lightness and good grace. But the harsh reality that the unionist-nationalist antagonism shows no signs of diminution suggests otherwise.

The institutions were indeed established on foot of the agreement, principally the 108-member New Northern Ireland Assembly, elected by single-transferable vote in June 1998. The result suggested a 'Balkanisation' of the region's politics into four principal pillars: republican (SF), constitutional-nationalist (SDLP), constitutional-unionist (UUP) and fundamentalist (DUP). Worrying for supporters of the agreement, not only was SF breathing down the neck of the SDLP but, of more immediate concern, Mr Trimble's party had performed so badly that he relied on the support of two 'loyalist' representatives to sustain a majority in the unionist bloc in the assembly. This was important not only morally but also because the combined election of Mr Trimble as first minister and his SDLP deputy, Séamus Mallon, as deputy in July relied on a 'parallel consent' vote supported by majorities in both blocs. And, over time, defections were further to weaken the UUP leader's position.

Other parts of the architecture remaining in the gift of Westminster, such as the Northern Ireland Human Rights Commission and the Equality Commission, were also put in place, following the legislative expression of the agreement in the Northern Ireland Act 1998. More seriously for Mr Trimble's position, the release of paramilitary prisoners began as early as September 1998, with no sign of the reciprocal movement implied in the agreement towards paramilitary weapons decommissioning. The key governmental structure, the four-party Executive Committee, was to have been set up using the d'Hondt proportionality rule. But, along with the consequent North/South Ministerial Council and British-Irish Council, its establishment was snagged by the impasse over decommissioning until December 1999, when power was finally transferred (though the two DUP members refused to attend meetings).

Devolution initially survived for only ten weeks, however, when it became clear that the inter-party 'understanding' held by some to have ended the deadlock was not mutually understood at all. Renewed intergovernmental effort brought about a commitment by the IRA to have some of its arms inspected by independent observers, and this was enough to secure the narrowest of majorities in Mr Trimble's party for the re-establishment of the executive at the end of May 2000. This time, the DUP adopted a revolving-door approach – not only not attending executive meetings but periodically reshuffling their two ministerial representatives.

The difficulty is that the limits of institutionalism lie in the absence of trust between the parties – an absence cruelly exposed in July 2000 in a bizarre exchange of claims and denials about resignation involving Mr Trimble and Mr Mallon. This arose from their failure to agree about the new name for the Royal Ulster Constabulary (Irish News, July 14th 2000, Irish Times, July 15th 2000), an issue kicked into touch at the time of the Belfast Agreement but which provoked renewed sectarian division when returned to play by Chris Patten, after his commission's report in autumn 1999.

Securing the settlement

■ **T**he best hope for success is the potential dawning of realisation that democratic self-government for Northern Ireland is the only show in town. The ideological arguments, which pitched a United Kingdom versus a United Ireland, had the decided drawback that the tug of war could only be arbitrated by the two 'national' governments. In practice, that left Northern Ireland a victim of a 'democratic deficit' in which all its elected representatives were disempowered and its citizens – whether British or Irish by choice – were, in effect, disenfranchised.

But this seems to rely on an acceptance that intercommunal co-existence is a cultural enrichment rather than a threat. Better to enjoy relationships of dialogue with one's neighbour, even if on occasions that means deferring to his or her sensibilities. The bitterness of the argument over flags over Stormont, and over parades on the streets, suggests Northern Ireland has some way to go before that happy state is reached.

Part of the process of getting there is a reaching out beyond the 'narrow ground' of the six counties to wider Irish, British and European horizons. What has driven the conflict in Northern Ireland has essentially been the view that identity and allegiance is an either/or decision. Yet Northern Ireland has no future if devolution becomes involution. It has much to gain, economically and socially, from co-ordination with the 'Celtic Tiger' with which it shares the island. It has much to learn, in policy terms, from participating in wider UK policy networks at a time of 'home rule all round'. And it has much more benefit to draw from its engagement, as a region with recognised special needs, with the European Union.

Meantime, a more prosaic, immediate task was the agreement of a Programme for Government. Focus groups run by Democratic Dialogue in 1999 showed a public yearning for indications of politicians abjuring adversarial rhetoric and co-operating on 'bread and butter' issues. Agreement in October 2000 on its draft content represented an important fillip for confidence amongst the people of Northern Ireland that the region was, finally, turning a corner.

Bibliography

Guelke, A (1988), Northern Ireland: The International Perspective, Dublin: Gill and Macmillan

Hayes, B and McAllister, I (1999), 'Ethnonationalism: public opinion and the Good Friday agreement', in Todd, J and Ruane, J eds, After the Good Friday Agreement: Analysing Political Change in Northern Ireland, Dublin: University College, pp 30-48

Kaldor, M (1999), New and Old Wars: Organized Violence in a Global Era, Cambridge: Polity Press

historical background

1

Home rule and the Ulster crisis

Paul Bew

■ The union of Great Britain and Ireland in 1800 undoubtedly reflected what would be called today a selfish strategic interest on the part of Britain. British statesmen openly confessed to having been shocked and frightened by the French invasion of 1798 in support of the revolt of the United Irishmen. The scale of the crisis exposed the inadequacy of the Irish parliament, and its inability to provide a framework for the development of an Irish society visibly tearing itself apart amid bitter sectarian recrimination.

In the mind of the prime minister, William Pitt, an idea formed. His thinking went beyond purely strategic considerations: he was influenced by Edmund Burke's critique of Protestant ascendancy. A union based on religious equality and economic growth was the solution to Ireland's problem. But the religious equality was to be delayed a generation until Catholic emancipation in 1829 – and, even then, only conceded because of the pressure generated by mass agitation. The economic growth came to Ireland, but it came in the main to the Protestant north-east; Catholic Ireland in the south and west endured the famine of 1846-50 in which a million people died.

These experiences explain the appeal of populist nationalism in 19th-century Ireland. They also explain why northern Protestants and Presbyterians – for whom the union essentially worked as advertised – turned away from the significant interest in separatist ideas which had marked the 1790s and instead supported the union. The 1885 general election revealed the political topography of sectarianism in a way that could not be ignored. The home-rulers led by Charles Stewart Parnell won every Irish seat with a Catholic preponderance, which meant every seat in the three southern provinces but two (the two Dublin university seats) and half those in Ulster.

The 'voice' of Ireland having spoken for home rule in this way, it is not surprising that the Liberal prime minister, William Gladstone, should have introduced a bill to restore a Dublin parliament with control over domestic Irish affairs but without a capacity for independent foreign policy. Since 1882 Gladstone had been inclined in this direction; he had been genuinely disturbed by the illiberal methods employed by his government to suppress the Land League – methods which had included the internment of 1,000 'suspects'.

But Gladstone's treatment of unionist, or more particularly Liberal Unionist, Ulster is a surprise. He now told his Belfast Liberal supporters – who had castigated him for his anti-Catholic pamphlets of the mid-1870s – that they were bigots if they did not return to the late 18th-century nationalist traditions of their community, or at any rate part of it. More practically, it seems likely Gladstone would have accepted, in both 1886 and 1893, some form of exclusion of north-east Ulster as the price of home rule for the rest of the island. But the debate never crystallised around exclusion because his government fell apart over the issue in 1886 and the Lords vetoed home rule when it finally passed the 'lower' house in 1893.

The key issue for Irish nationalists was how to interpret this last defeat. John Dillon, who led the majority of nationalist MPs – those who had opposed Parnell in the divorce crisis of 1890 – felt that the way forward lay in a campaign against the Lords veto. John Redmond, leader of the Parnellite minority, argued rather differently: Redmond claimed that the Lords could only act as it did because a large segment of UK public opinion was worried about the treatment of the large Protestant minority in any home-rule Ireland. He drew on Parnell's own late concerns on this matter and argued for an explicit policy of 'toleration' of Protestants, demonstrating to English public opinion that nationalism was genuinely non-sectarian and that all would be well – and, anyway, the Lords was too entrenched to be challenged for a generation or more.

By 1910, however, Redmond, now the leader of Irish nationalism, had, in effect, changed his mind. He involved himself in a successful campaign, exploiting the nationalist balance of power at Westminster, to destroy the Lords veto and, less successfully, impose home rule on the whole island, regardless of Protestant opinion. In 1912 the Liberal government apparently went along with this; in its heart it was merely waiting for the inevitable Ulster Protestant revolt of 1912-14 – sometimes illegal but also avoiding loss of life – to force Redmond to a compromise, involving at least a temporary partition.

In early 1916 Redmond was supremely self-confident: he was sure there would be a Dublin parliament as soon as the war ended and, at worst, a partitioned area in the north-east would be ruled directly by London with a pro-Catholic input from his own party which could expect to control the Dublin cabinet and be represented in the Westminster one. His benign scenario was disrupted by the insurrectionists who launched the Easter rising of 1916, who insisted that only a united Irish republic was a satisfactory solution. Several thousand, mainly Irish, deaths later, these forces accepted partition: dominion status rather than a republic and what came to be known as a 'Protestant parliament for a Protestant people' in the north.

In this context, however, it is worth noting the verdict of Stephen Gwynn, nationalist MP for Galway from 1908 to 1918: 'Sinn Féin honeycombed the British service in Ireland with persons who thought it honest to conspire actively against the government which paid them. One can not expect Sir James Craig and his ministers to have forgotten that, nor blame them for acting on the memory.'

2

Partition and the failure of majoritarianism
Paul Dixon

'Fifty years of Unionist misrule'

■ There are strongly contrasting unionist and nationalist accounts of the period of Stormont government from 1921 to 1972. Republicans have exaggerated the abuses of this Unionist period to justify their violence, while unionists have downplayed them to delegitimise the grievances of the civil rights movement and nationalist arguments for Irish unity.

The Government of Ireland Act 1920, which partitioned Ireland, was an unhappy compromise between unionist and nationalist interests, and was widely seen as a temporary measure until Ireland could be reunited. It established two equal Irish parliaments and a Council of Ireland which would promote co-operation between north and south, with a view to eventual reunification. Republicans and nationalists tended to believe Ireland would be reunited as an independent state. The British and unionists, meanwhile, looked forward to a united Ireland more closely tied to Britain, through a closer relationship within the empire/Commonwealth or even the re-entry of Ireland into the UK.

The British government sought to insulate itself from the troublesome 'Irish question'. The Stormont parliament was imposed on unionists and vested with considerable autonomy and power over domestic public policy, including law and order. A Speaker's convention emerged at Westminster which prevented the discussion of affairs held to be the responsibility of the devolved government. As a result, there was little oversight of Northern Ireland affairs – even though section 75 of the Government of Ireland Act preserved 'the supreme authority of the parliament of the UK over all persons, matters and things in Northern Ireland'.

The government's determination to distance itself from Irish affairs clashed with its attempt to protect minority rights in Northern Ireland. Proportional representation had been introduced for Stormont and local elections – a departure from the British first-past-the-post system – to improve minority representation. But the Ulster Unionist Party consolidated its dominance by abolishing PR, first for local elections and then for Stormont. This step weakened nationalist opposition to the UUP but also the challenge from labourists and populist 'loyalists'.

London initially resisted the Unionist move, withholding consent from the Stormont Bill abolishing PR. But when the Unionist cabinet threatened to resign, thereby precipitating a constitutional crisis and a reopening of the 'Irish question', it backed down. The Unionists soon came to realise the advantage of having their own government and parliament, as a means of safeguarding their interests against both nationalists and a perfidious British government.

The abolition of PR for local elections in 1922 and the gerry-mandering of local-government boundaries underpinned much of the subsequent discrimination, shifting the control of some authorities to unionists even where Catholics were in a majority. There is little doubt that there was anti-Catholic discrimination; the debate revolves around the extent of such (intentional and unintentional) discrimination. There is also evidence of some discrimination against Protestants. Discrimination was defended on the grounds that the Catholic minority represented an 'enemy within', who could not be trusted in a time of emergency. But even when the emergency passed discrimination continued, and little attempt was made to win Catholic support for the Northern Ireland state.

Limits of the Westminster model

■ The Westminster model of democracy compounded the problem of Catholic exclusion. This model usually concentrates power in the hands of the leadership of one party, which is not constrained by a codified constitution or a clear separation of powers between executive, judiciary and legislature. Although the ideal is the alternation of political parties in government, the reality has often been protracted one-party rule (the Conservatives during the inter-war period, Conservatives 1951-64, Labour 1964-70 and 1974-79, Conservatives 1979-97). Such one-party dominance has attracted criticism from both the left and right in British politics.

The dominance of the UUP was demonstrated by its victory in every election from 1921 to 1972. Opposition parties – labourist, loyalist or nationalist – were permanently excluded from power. Unionist governments had little Protestant working-class representation, were dominated by members of the Orange Order and gave no role to Catholics. They were able simply to ignore the Opposition – the Wild Birds Act was the latter's sole legislative achievement during the period of untrammelled Unionist power.

The government of Northern Ireland did, when it suited its interests, diverge substantially from the standards and legislation operating in the rest of the UK. Such asymmetry may be appropriate in a unique part of the state which contains a large minority which aspires to be part of a different state and does not subscribe to the dominant identity.

Cold war

■ **D**uring the 'cold war' between north and south, between 1921 and 1965, the south did little to try to win Protestant support for unity. While historians have rightly highlighted the sectarian nature of the Northern Ireland state in the 30s, others have argued that a southern shift to more sectarian positions produced a northern response.

During the 30s relations between Northern Ireland and the Irish Free State polarised. As Unionist leaders infamously declared the north a Protestant polity, nationalists in the south underlined the Free State's Catholicism. James Craig, the prime minister of Northern Ireland (1921-40), declared: 'In the south they boasted of a Catholic state. They still boast of southern Ireland being a Catholic state. All I boast of is that we are a Protestant parliament and a Protestant state.' In 1933 Sir Basil Brooke, future prime minister, claimed Catholics were trying to 'destroy the power and constitution of Ulster' and appealed to loyalists 'to employ good Protestant lads and lassies'.

The victory of the anti-treaty and 'slightly constitutional' Fianna Fáil party in the 1932 Free State elections brought Eamon de Valera to power. De Valera's protectionism and the advent of a 'trade war' between Britain and the Free State resulted in a decline of cross-border trade. Some nationalists believed that a prosperous southern economy, rather than cross-border trade, could attract unionists into a united Ireland. The Catholic priorities of the Free State were becoming more apparent, British heritage was dismantled and Protestants in the south claimed persecution: their numbers had dropped 32 per cent between 1911 and 1926. This process culminated in the 1937 constitution, which enshrined the special position of the Catholic Church. Irish neutrality during world war two and the declaration of the republic in 1948 underscored the polarisation between north and south.

This 'cold war' consolidated the position of Unionism. An apparently friendly government in the republic might have increased British pressure to make concessions and reach accommodation with the south. The thaw in north-south relations, signified in 1965 by the first meeting of the two premiers in 40 years, correspondingly raised unionist fears and British hopes that Irish reunification might at last be returning to the political agenda.

The challenge of civil rights

■ During the early 60s a campaign for civil rights emerged which became a mass movement when its second march, in Derry, was attacked by the Royal Ulster Constabulary on October 5th 1968. There are three main perspectives on the emergence of the movement. Its leaders claimed their campaign was an attempt to end discriminatory practices, ensure political equality for all and win 'British rights for British citizens'. They denied it had anything to do with the border question. The civil-rights movement exhausted constitutional methods for redress and finally took to the streets.

The Unionist government alleged that the movement had little to do with 'alleged' abuses of civil rights but was a republican/communist tactic to bring about a united Ireland in keeping with previous anti-partition campaigns. There was republican involvement in the establishment of the civil-rights movement and many activists shared a nationalist perspective. But there is little evidence to suggest that those republicans and communists who were involved in the civil rights movement predicted the reaction their campaign would bring.

The third perspective focuses on the post-war growth of the state as an explanation. This growth resulted in increased competition for the expanding resources it distributed. The civil-rights campaign raised issues about the allocation of public housing, discrimination in public employment and the siting of public institutions. This argument suggests that the thrust of the civil-rights movement was from below, drawing its strength from growing conflict over discrimination, access to state resources and the impoverishment of the Catholic working class.

Spiral into violence

■ The spontaneous mobilisation of large sections of the Catholic community after the Derry march and the difficulty leaders of the civil-rights movement had in controlling this explosion indicated the discontent within the community and the bottom-up thrust of the movement. Violent confrontations between marchers and the RUC expanded the scope of grievance to include the sensitive issue of security reform. The publicity generated by the confrontations (so resonant of clashes in the US) finally brought swift action by the British government to see that the civil-rights demands were met.

After October 1968 there may have been an increasing feeling, encouraged by the actions of the republic's government and the mass Catholic mobilisation in the north, that the republican movement's opportunity to end the partition of Ireland had finally arrived. It had every incentive to provoke further conflict with the state which, partly through its repression and over-reaction, helped eventually to re-establish Irish reunification on the British political agenda.

3

Direct rule and the 'democratic deficit'
Sydney Elliott

Reluctant governors

■ **W**ithin six years a stable but contested political system in Northern Ireland went through civil disorder from 1968, a régime change in 1972 and the collapse of a new system in 1974. The absence of support for political integration with the UK or the Republic of Ireland meant the focus returned to finding an acceptable form of devolved government. The principles derived from the new thinking of 1972-4 – power sharing and an 'Irish dimension' – were applied in varying degrees to several abortive attempts over the next quarter century until the Belfast agreement.

The Achilles heel of the old Stormont system, its contested legitimacy, was exposed by the civil-rights movement. Serious violence in the summer of 1969 and increasing opposition alienation put large question-marks over the devolved parliament. The British government considered the introduction of direct rule but at that point decided against. There was an element of doubt about its feasibility and some ministers and constitutional lawyers regarded Northern Ireland's position as closer to dominion status than devolution.

The need for army support for the police from August 1969 brought, however, a change in the relationship between Stormont and Whitehall. An army commander took charge of security operations and a new post of British government representative was established, so that Westminster would have its own watchdog at Stormont (next door to the prime minister). Thereafter, whatever the powers or inclination of the Northern Ireland government, it could not resist requests for change from Westminster.

Worsening security – especially after the failure of internment, introduced in August 1971 – revived speculation about direct rule. Actions by the army made the decision inevitable. The shooting dead of two men in Derry in July 1971 and the refusal of an inquiry had seen the nationalist opposition at Stormont walk out. The shooting dead of 14 civilians at a march in Derry on 'Bloody Sunday' in January 1972 brought it closer. On March 24th the prime minister, Edward Heath, said he had proposed periodic border polls in Northern Ireland, a start to phasing out internment and the transfer of security powers. When the latter was refused by the Northern Ireland government, the Stormont parliament was prorogued and direct rule instituted.

It was an act that pleased anti-unionists, but horrified even the most moderate of unionists. The speed with which it was accomplished – 51 years of self-government wrapped up after 30 hours debate in the Commons – was ostensibly a lesson in the subordinate nature of the Northern Ireland Parliament. But it was achieved with the compliance of the Unionist government and a legal challenge was never attempted.

Northern Ireland now had its own secretary of state, similar to Scotland and Wales, and the first holder of the office was William Whitelaw, a senior Conservative politician, assisted by a small team of junior ministers. Northern Ireland was governed under a Temporary Provisions Act, and legislation was brought forward as orders in council, which could not be amended on the floor of the Commons. In an attempt to make direct rule more palatable, Mr Whitelaw set up an Advisory Commission, but it was boycotted by unionists: Brian (later Lord) Faulkner, Northern Ireland's last prime minister, complained of being treated 'like a coconut colony'.

Power-sharing

■ **N**ew thinking was required on how to reconstruct a system of government. There was some consideration of the main ideas of 'consociationalism', as set out by Arend Lijphart. In essence, these were drawn from other divided societies with a view to creating stability until longer-term relationships could be worked out. The main elements to replace majoritarianism were: power-sharing or élite accommodation, segmental autonomy, proportionality and mutual veto or concurrent majority.

The first attempt to engage the Northern Ireland parties was at the Darlington conference in September 1972 but only pro-union parties attended. A month later a discussion paper, The Future of Northern Ireland, stated a preference for a union based on consent, incorporation of the minority into the executive and (the first explicit mention) an 'Irish dimension'. A white paper, Northern Ireland Constitutional Proposals, followed in March 1973.

Also in March was held what was envisaged as the first of periodic referenda to test opinion on Northern Ireland's constitutional status vis-á-vis the UK and the republic. This was in the hope of taking the border out of day-to-day politics but the referendum was vitiated by a nationalist boycott and was not repeated. Northern Ireland was given a 78-member assembly, elected in June by proportional representation (single transferable vote), with the object of giving minorities a bigger chance of representation and participation in government. The scheme was embodied in the Northern Ireland Constitution Act of 1973, which also abolished the office of governor. Three parties, the Ulster Unionist Party, the Social Democratic and Labour Party and Alliance, agreed on a power-sharing administration in November. Early in December, at Sunningdale, the executive parties and ministers from the London and Dublin governments agreed an Irish dimension including a north-south Council of Ireland.

The new coalition took office on January 1st 1974, having being sworn in by a new secretary of state, Francis Pym. It comprised five Unionist, three SDLP and one Alliance under the leadership of a chief executive, Mr Faulkner (Unionist) and a deputy chief executive, Gerry Fitt (SDLP). Two other SDLP, one Alliance and one Unionist were also members of the wider administration.

The new dispensation rapidly ran into trouble. On January 4th Mr Faulkner was defeated in the Ulster Unionist Council, his party's governing body, over endorsement of the Sunningdale agreement; he resigned as party leader. The administration had a majority in the assembly but faced virulent opposition from loyalists. In a general election in February candidates from three anti-power-sharing unionist groups, gathered under the banner of the United Ulster Unionist Council, polled 51 per cent of the votes and won 11 of 12 Northern Ireland seats. The new Labour secretary of state, Merlyn Rees, tried to defend the region's institutions but a loyalist strike – aimed against power sharing and the Council of Ireland – led to the resignation in May of the Unionist members of the executive, and the collapse of the administration.

Direct rule renewed

■ **D**irect rule was resumed – the fourth change of administration in two years. Legal authority was provided by the Northern Ireland Act of 1974, which provided for the government of Northern Ireland by Westminster ministers, subject to annual renewal. The assembly was prorogued.

The Labour government moved quickly to try to break the political deadlock and reinstate the assembly. In July 1974 it announced that the region's political parties were to be given the opportunity to produce a viable constitution, rather than have one imposed. A 78-member Constitutional Convention was elected in May 1975, with an independent chair. The government confined itself to shaping opinion through three papers: on finance and the economy, on suggested procedures and some historical precedents and on Northern Ireland as a divided society. The majority report by the UUUC parties proposed majority rule and no Irish dimension. It was rejected by Parliament, which had the 1974 model in mind. A suggested emergency voluntary coalition split the Vanguard section of the UUUC but, when the convention was briefly recalled in March 1976, opinions had not changed and it was abandoned.

In its aftermath, the government sought to widen consultation, outside and inside Parliament, on Northern Ireland legislation. A Northern Ireland Committee of MPs was set up to allow general debates on policy. Draft orders were shown in advance to the Northern Ireland parties. The aim of this period of direct rule seemed to be to harmonise the region's policy and legislation with that of the rest of the UK. Some departments established for the convenience of the executive were dropped and others merged to produce eight. After James Callaghan became prime minister in 1976, the government accepted there was a case for more than 12 Northern Ireland MPs – a long-standing unionist claim. The idea was endorsed by the Speaker's conference in 1978, in the face of SDLP opposition.

The British government did not rush into any new initiative. In November 1977 Roy Mason, as secretary of state, put forward a tentative plan for discussion by the parties, but the initial exchanges did not suggest any agreement. The SDLP in particular rejected the absence of an Irish dimension and the party adopted a 'British withdrawal' motion, retreating from its pursuit of agreement within Northern Ireland. At the same time, the Conservative opposition was urging that the priority should be local-government reform – a course frequently urged by unionists. The SDLP feared this would lead to unionist domination, a view the secretary of state indicated he endorsed.

The Conservative government elected in May 1979 at first appeared committed to its manifesto proposals for a regional council or councils for Northern Ireland, with a wide range of powers over local services. But after the death of Airey Neave (with whom the policy was identified) at the hands of an INLA bomb in the Commons car park, the policy changed. A twin-track position was developed amid increasing pressure from the US.

First, the new secretary of state, Humphrey Atkins, sought to establish whether a basis existed for devolution. After the publication of a white paper, Proposals for Further Discussion, he called the four main parties to a Constitutional Conference seeking 'the highest level of agreement ... which will best meet the needs of Northern Ireland'. The main unionist party did not attend, the SDLP was divided on participation and by November 1980 there was no agreement. Although in July 1981 Mr Atkins proposed to create an advisory council of MPs, MEPs and other elected representatives, the proposal was lost in the intercommunal tension surrounding the H-block hunger strike.

The second track began in December 1980 with a unique, high-level meeting of British and Irish ministers in Dublin. In a serious effort to improve UK-republic relations, a series of joint studies was instigated on security, mutual understanding, citizens' rights, economic co-operation and possible new institutional structures. In 1981 an Anglo-Irish Intergovernmental Council was created as a forum for discussion, with provision for a parliamentary tier. While relations deteriorated during the Falklands crisis of 1982, an institution for mutual contact had been established.

'Rolling devolution'

■ **D**espite the experience of his predecessor, the new secretary of state, James Prior – the most senior politician to hold the post since William Whitelaw – was willing to put his reputation on the line 'to get political progress'. At first he investigated the possibilities of an assembly with ministers from the region nominated by himself, and a separation of administrative and legislative responsibility on the US model. But he settled on the idea of 'rolling devolution', where an assembly would start with only a consultative and scrutiny role. This could be extended to embrace the devolution of one or more departments, but this would depend on achievement in the assembly of 'cross-community support'. The small group of cabinet ministers who settled Northern Ireland policy saw it as a means of getting more political support for security policy, and of giving a semblance of stability to attract outside investment (unemployment was running at around 20 per cent).

The scheme that eventually emerged in early 1982 was based, as in 1973, on a 78-seat assembly elected by PR (STV) in the 12 Westminster constituencies. The Devolution Bill provided that the assembly could apply to Westminster for devolved powers if 70 per cent of members backed it. The Bill also provided that the assembly could discuss regional legislation and set up scrutiny committees for the by now six Stormont departments, and an amendment allowed for a non-statutory security committee.

Predictably, the reaction was mixed. The UUP and DUP rejected the weighted-majority provision as a revived power-sharing requirement, although the DUP was more attracted than the UUP to the initial scrutiny powers. To Alliance it was a last chance for Northern Ireland to solve its own problems. The SDLP regarded the scheme as 'unworkable' and an 'expensive charade' (views echoed by the Fianna Fáil government in the republic). Sinn Féin, contesting a Stormont election for the first time, sought to displace the SDLP as the main voice of nationalists and win political support for its 'Brits out' approach. Around 20 right-wing Conservative MPs mounted a filibuster and argued that the 1979 manifesto should be implemented. But the measure was put through without difficulty after a 'guillotine' (unusual for a constitutional bill) had been applied.

With both the SDLP and SF fighting on an abstentionist platform, although differing on the issue of violence, the government's hopes for the assembly were distinctly limited. The SDLP secured 14 seats and SF a surprising five, so that only 59 members attended the opening session. The absence of SDLP members obviously made it impossible to achieve the cross-community support necessary for devolution. The main work of the assembly was, therefore, the scrutiny of government departments and advice on draft legislation.

In 1985, the new secretary of state, Douglas Hurd, reverted to the London-Dublin axis, responding to the report of the New Ireland Forum – established by the republic's government to forge a nationalist consensus – in 1984. Negotiations between the two capitals led to the Anglo-Irish Agreement of that November.

The Anglo-Irish Agreement

■ **T**he response outside Northern Ireland to what was represented as the settlement of an historic difference was a general, if not effusive, welcome. Within the region, nationalists gave it immediate support, growing in strength as they witnessed unionist discomfiture at the hands of a former political friend in the Conservative Party. Unionist rage at the role given to the republic in the 'internal affairs' of part of the UK crossed all classes and shades of opinion and was reflected in a range of protests, from huge rallies outside Belfast City Hall to boycotts of district-council business – in general trying to demonstrate that unionist consent did not extend to this 'joint rule'. The assembly became a platform for protest, leading to a withdrawal by the Alliance members. The NIO withdrew committee staff and access to departments and papers, and the assembly was dissolved in June 1986 – some of its protesting members being carried by police from the building.

The assembly, however limited by nationalist abstention, did enable members to exercise a representative function absent since 1974. It held 221 plenary sessions and 426 witnesses gave evidence to it. The scrutiny committees prepared 118 reports, containing 998 recommendations of which two-thirds were accepted; they also had an input into draft legislation. The passing of the assembly did not diminish the need to subject the direct-rule régime to political and administrative accountability.

Despite the commitment of the signatories of the Anglo-Irish Agreement to devolution (article 4), no new proposal was made. The expectation of government – that, once the overarching framework of relations between the UK and the republic was established, devolution would follow naturally – proved facile. Unionists, with two electoral mandates behind them, in 1986 (when they resigned their Westminster seats and all bar one was re-elected) and 1987 (in the general election), could not accept devolution under the agreement framework.

After the June 1987 election the unionist leaders, James Molyneaux (UUP) and Rev Ian Paisley (DUP) engaged in 'talks about talks' with the secretary of state on the principle of suspending the Intergovernmental Conference established by the agreement to enable inter-party talks. Early in 1988 outline proposals were submitted which had not even produced a detailed reply by the end of the year. The secretary of state also held talks with other parties, including the SDLP, but without any indication that the 'widespread acceptance' criterion for devolution had been established. Further, soon after the unionist proposals, the SDLP began private meetings with SF, which set back any possibility of direct talks with unionists. SDLP representatives also said the party was not committed to devolution in principle, but only in so far as it would contribute to solving a problem they identified as one of 'relationships'.

Interestingly, the republic's government appeared keener to facilitate new discussions than the comparative satisfaction shown by the then secretary of state, Tom King, suggested. His successor, Peter Brooke, however launched an effort for inter-party talks and devolution in January 1990. The general aim was a more broadly based structure than the Anglo-Irish Agreement.

4

The 90s 'talks' and 'peace' processes

Duncan Morrow

The aftermath of the Anglo-Irish Agreement

■ **W**hile the Anglo-Irish Agreement of 1985 did not generate the momentum towards a lasting political settlement to which its supporters aspired, it quickly became embedded as a central plank of direct rule. Although the agreement had only limited impact on day-to day experience, it was the clearest indicator yet of the limits of the unionist veto and the evolving direction of governmental thinking in London and Dublin. Further, it represented a triumph for John Hume and his Social Democratic and Labour Party. The experience of being sidelined traumatised the leadership of the Ulster Unionist Party and was to shape party responses to the negotiations which evolved through the 90s.

Unionist opposition to the Anglo-Irish Agreement, so impressive as a rejectionist front in 1986, was deeply divided when it came to alternative strategies. A vocal minority campaigned for 'full integration' into the UK, with the organisation of British political parties in Northern Ireland. This divided them sharply from the Democratic Unionist Party, which had no coherent allies at Westminster, and even from the UUP, led by James Molyneaux, who had no intention after 1985 of leaving the defence of the union to British Conservatives.

Unionists were not the only group for whom the Anglo-Irish Agreement created difficulties. In bolstering the SDLP and constitutional nationalism, the political momentum which Sinn Féin had generated after the hunger strikes was effectively halted. Poor election results in the republic in 1987 and widespread outrage over the Enniskillen bomb, led some republicans, including the SF leader, Gerry Adams, to review political and military tactics. In 1988, the SDLP and SF leaderships conducted a series of meetings and exchanged a variety of documents. Although these ended without agreement, especially on the role of Britain in the conflict in Northern Ireland, formal political contact was established on a new basis. By 1990, there were clear indications that both unionists and republicans were anxious to find new strategies.

Talks and secret talks

■ Peter Brooke's arrival as Northern Ireland secretary was the catalyst for a new chapter. Over 14 months, Mr Brooke conducted bilateral 'talks about talks' with the main constitutional parties, with a view to establishing a basis on which unionists could re-enter formal political negotiations. By June 1991, the four largest constitutional parties (UUP, SDLP, DUP and Alliance) had agreed to attend talks sponsored by the two governments, on the basis that 'nothing is agreed until everything is agreed'. To satisfy unionist sensitivities, meetings of the British-Irish Intergovernmental Conference (established under the Anglo-Irish Agreement) were suspended for the duration.

The agenda was to be based on three distinct 'strands' of negotiation:

internal arrangements for Northern Ireland, north-south relations and relations between the UK and the republic. Although the talks were suspended within three weeks, they established that Ulster Unionism was leaving behind the fundamental opposition which had characterised the late 80s.

Even more radically, Mr Brooke took seriously the indications of changing thinking in the leadership of SF. Convinced that conflict in Northern Ireland could not be resolved by military means alone, he accepted that communication with republicans, although difficult, would ultimately be essential. The condition, however, was IRA willingness to end its campaign of violence. By way of indicating this shift in British strategy, the secretary of state declared (Taylor, 1998: 318): 'The British Government has no selfish strategic or economic interest in Northern Ireland: our role is to help, enable and encourage …' In early 1991, he authorised tentative secret discussions between the intelligence services and the leading republican Martin McGuinness. Despite the IRA's spectacular mortar bomb attack on 10 Downing Street and a deterioration in security in Northern Ireland, the talks through intermediaries continued.

On the day after the British general election in spring 1992, the IRA exploded a huge bomb outside the Baltic Exchange in the City, causing damage estimated at £800 million. The following day, Sir Patrick Mayhew was appointed to replace Mr Brooke as Northern Ireland secretary. To facilitate a return to the stalled talks of 1991, the workings of the intergovernmental conference were once more suspended, for three months.

Although the subsequent talks were detailed and intense, especially between the UUP and SDLP, they came to a halt by November amid considerable recrimination. Unionists were dismayed that understandings reached between negotiators at Stormont were rejected by the SDLP leadership, particularly Mr Hume. Yet although the talks were a failure, they left an important legacy. Both the negotiation formula ('nothing is agreed until everything is agreed') and the three-strand agenda were to reappear as the core principles governing the talks leading to the Belfast Agreement of 1998.

The beginning of the end?

■ **F**ollowing the collapse of the talks, government interest shifted from enticing unionism back into political dialogue towards attempting to bring SF into direct negotiations. By November 1992, Mr Hume believed from his continuing contacts with Mr Adams that new talks involving the republicans were possible and offered the best chance of long-term stability. The republic's government, now led by Albert Reynolds, actively encouraged these developments. Sir Patrick indicated in a speech in Coleraine (Northern Ireland Information Service, December 16th 1992) that SF could expect to be admitted to talks in the event of 'a genuine and established cessation of violence'.

Without informing other political actors, British intelligence intensified its contacts with the IRA. At the same time, the Hume-Adams dialogue was translated by Dublin into a peace proposal and presented to London by Mr Reynolds as a 'starting point for negotiation'. All movement towards negotiation, however, was constantly challenged by paramilitary activity on the ground. When security deteriorated drastically in the autumn of 1993, both governments intensified their efforts to achieve a political breakthrough. In a flurry of diplomatic activity, and to the alarm of many unionists, the taoiseach and the prime minister, John Major, agreed on December 15th a joint statement on the future of Northern Ireland, known universally as the Downing Street Declaration.

Although the declaration substantially restated the core of the Anglo-Irish Agreement, there were significant changes aimed at enticing republicans into talks without alienating unionists. The document repeated Mr Brooke's declaration about British interests in

Ireland and accepted the principle of self-determination on the island. Nevertheless, the declaration made clear that self-determination was to be 'on the basis of consent, freely and concurrently given, North and South ...' In contrast to the aftermath of the Anglo-Irish Agreement, the UUP reacted calmly. Republicans, on the other hand, were less than pleased, regarding the document as a retreat from the conclusions of the Hume-Adams dialogue. While a declaration signed by a Fianna Fáil taoiseach with a Conservative prime minister and enthusiastically supported in Washington could not be ignored, it took a further nine months of violence, 'clarification' and political pressure from Dublin and Washington before the IRA called a 'complete cessation of military operations' on August 31st 1994.

The cease-fire was applauded internationally and greeted with delight by nationalists in Ireland. The republic's government moved quickly to integrate SF into the nationalist mainstream, organising a photo-call embracing Messrs Reynolds, Hume and Adams and announcing a Forum for Peace and Reconciliation to explore the opportunities for progress. Unionists, on the other hand, were sceptical – pointing to the absence of the word 'permanent' in the IRA declaration – or hostile. Seeking to reassure them, Mr Major underlined that there would be no change in the constitutional status of Northern Ireland without the express agreement of its main political parties, the parliaments in London and Dublin and the people of Northern Ireland in a referendum. In the context of this 'triple lock', with the claim that 'the union is safe' the loyalist paramilitaries announced their own cease-fire, conditional on the maintenance of that by the IRA (Bew and Gillespie, 1996).

The long road to dialogue

■ The cease-fire created enormous expectations within Northern Ireland and beyond. Nevertheless, it was clear from an early stage that the basis for talks involving all shades of opinion did not yet exist.

The Forum for Peace and Reconciliation met without unionist participation. Unionists refused to countenance direct dialogue with SF without a start to IRA decommissioning. This the IRA, supported by the loyalists, resolutely refused to contemplate, regarding it as tantamount to surrender.

The precariousness of the process was illustrated graphically by early 1995. In February, the two governments published the so-called Frameworks Documents, putting into print their initial proposals for political institutions. These were angrily rejected by the UUP, and widely interpreted as a disaster for Mr Molyneaux's strategy of seeking to influence the British government through private consultations at Westminster. When, one month later, Sir Patrick announced in Washington that the government regarded decommissioning as a precondition for the opening of political talks with SF, republicans were in despair. By the autumn, the UUP leadership had fallen into the hands of David Trimble, thought to be the most inflexible of the available candidates, and the IRA cease-fire was under severe strain.

In an attempt to resolve the situation in advance of a planned visit to Northern Ireland by the US president, Bill Clinton, the two governments asked the former US senator George Mitchell to chair an ad hoc commission on decommissioning. In January 1996, the commission reported that all participants in talks should commit themselves: exclusively to democratic and peaceful means of resolving political issues, to the total disarmament of paramilitary organisations and to working 'constructively to achieve full and verifiable decommissioning as part of the process of all-party negotiations ...' Although deeply disappointed that the report did not demand prior decommissioning, the British government formally accepted it, but immediately agreed to a unionist demand that elections to a Northern Ireland Forum should now determine the popular mandate of the negotiators. Nationalists were outraged and within weeks the IRA had broken its cease-fire, with a huge explosion at Canary Wharf in London's docklands.

For 15 months, there was little sign of any movement towards talks. The elections in May 1996 proved a triumph for SF, which saw its share of the vote increase to 15 per cent. When an Orange Order march was blocked by police in Portadown, Co Armagh, in July, there was widespread mayhem in Protestant areas. When the decision to block the march was reversed under this pressure, there was serious rioting in Catholic areas. In protest, the SDLP withdrew from the forum established after the elections and community relations, so hopeful in 1994, were at a new low.

IRA activity in England reached a peak during the general election of 1997. Although stunts like the forced postponement of the Grand National race had only marginal influence on the election itself, the new Labour government was determined to inject impetus into the moribund 'peace process'. Once again, changes in the world beyond Northern Ireland were to prove decisive. In spite of paramilitary shootings and widespread tension over loyal-order parades, the IRA announced a renewal of its cease-fire on July 20th. The new Northern Ireland secretary, Marjorie ('Mo') Mowlam, assured SF there would be no further obstacles in the way of direct negotiations.

As before, the DUP refused to contemplate talks. But the UUP was clearly split. Although taken somewhat by surprise by the speed of events, Protestant business and church leaders called for unionists to take up the challenge. With some reservation, Mr Trimble agreed to participate in round-table talks, although refusing to meet SF in any bilateral context. On September 15th, with Mr Mitchell in the chair, multi-party talks involving both unionists and republicans opened at Stormont.

Bibliography

Bew, P and Gillespie, G (1996), The Northern Ireland Peace Process 1993-1996: A Chronology, London: Serif

Taylor, Peter (1998), Provos: the IRA and Sinn Fein, London: Bloomsbury

5
Negotiating the agreement

Henry Patterson

Parties and procedures

■ **A**lthough British policy-makers had for some time accepted the argument – put with particular emphasis by the Social Democratic and Labour Party leader, John Hume – that only 'inclusive' negotiations would be successful in Northern Ireland, there is no doubt that the decision by the Democratic Unionist Party and Bob McCartney's United Kingdom Unionist Party to leave the talks process when Sinn Féin entered in September 1997 was the sine qua non of ultimate success. As the talks chair, George Mitchell, puts it in his account (Mitchell, 1999: 110), 'Reaching agreement without their presence was extremely difficult, it would have been impossible with them in the room.'

The remaining participants were: on the unionist side the Ulster Unionist Party and the two small, paramilitary-linked parties, the Progressive Unionist Party and the Ulster Democratic Party; for nationalists the SDLP and SF; and a 'non-confessional' bloc containing the Alliance Party, the Northern Ireland Women's Coalition and a Labour grouping. Despite often conflicting agendas and mutual suspicions, the centre of gravity of the talks process would be the determination of the SDLP and the UUP to work together.

The format and agenda were similar to the multiparty talks of 1991-2, following the accepted 'three-strand' formula: strand one dealing with the internal government of Northern Ireland, strand two with north-south relations and strand three with 'east-west' (British-Irish). But the prerequisite of success in the three strands was a satisfactory conclusion to decades of unionist-nationalist and British-Irish contention over the basic constitutional issue of Northern Ireland's legitimacy as a political entity.

The SF president, Gerry Adams, writing in Ireland on Sunday on March 8th 1998, indicated that his party's 'bottom line' included the retention of articles 2 and 3 of the republic's constitution, which made a jurisdictional and territorial claim on Northern Ireland. But in their 'Heads of Agreement ' paper of January 12th the two premiers, Tony Blair and Bertie Ahern, had committed themselves to a 'balanced constitutional change'. While the UUP leader, David Trimble, rejected (Sunday Independent, March 8th 1998) any implied equivalence between articles 2 and 3 and section 75 of the 1920 Government of Ireland Act (which when promulgated claimed ultimate Westminster authority over all of Ireland), the substantive point – acceptance by the republic of the principle of consent – would be at the heart of the agreement.

Constitutional issues and north-south institutions

■ **U**nionist negotiators were acutely conscious of the degree to which ambiguity on Dublin's part on constitutional issues had been one of two main factors destroying what support there had been in the Protestant community in 1974 for the Sunningdale agreement. Given the presence this time of SF – a party that was still, in rhetorical terms at least, a revolutionary nationalist organisation – it was the willingness of the taoiseach to prioritise stability over his party's traditional republican aspirations that proved decisive. His good personal relations with Mr Trimble, and his awareness of the constraints upon the UUP leader and the need for any agreement to win the support of a clear referendum majority in a society where 60 per cent of the voters are unionist, led Mr Ahern to provide clear constitutional recognition of Northern Ireland. Yet, the price the republic's government and the SDLP wanted unionists to pay for recognition was a high one.

The Heads of Agreement paper had appeared to signal an acceptance by Mr Ahern that the north-south institutional structure envisaged in the Framework Document of 1995 – that of an ambitious, 'stand-alone' body which would be, in the words of David Andrews, minister for foreign affairs, 'a third government' on the island – had been scrapped in favour of a body that would bring together ministers whose executive powers were derived solely from the positions they held in a new Northern Ireland Assembly and the Dáil. The paper had also referred to a new east-west structure – the British-Irish Council. This would consist of representatives of the London and Dublin governments and regional/national administrations across the islands.

This appealed to unionists as reflecting their view that the agreement, unlike the Anglo-Irish Agreement, took the 'British Isles' – not the 'narrow ground' of Northern Ireland and its relationship with Dublin – as the relevant context. It also would allow unionists to treat any agreement as part of the broader process of devolution within the United Kingdom, and not a deal which would reinforce the north's image in the rest of the UK as 'a place apart'. In return, however, the republic's government, under considerable pressure from SF, returned to the ambitious vistas of the Framework Document.

In the early hours of the morning of the last Tuesday of the negotiations, April 7th 1998, Mr Mitchell delivered the first draft of the proposed agreement to the parties. The strand-two section – the subject of prolonged and heated discussion between the two governments – was, he recognised immediately, unlikely to be acceptable to Mr Trimble. Dublin concerns that a 'watered down' Framework Document would push Mr Adams and SF out of the talks appeared to have triumphed.

The draft was clear that the cross-border bodies had independent authority. With long annexes listing more than 60 cross-border schemes and bodies, this instantly confirmed unionist fears that the north-south dimension was part of a strategy of 'creeping reunification'. Both Lord Alderdice, leader of Alliance, and Mr Trimble called for the prime minister, Tony Blair, to come immediately to Belfast to salvage a deal.

Mr Blair's arrival on the Tuesday evening began a process of frenetic negotiations which would involve the two premiers, all the parties and, at crucial points, most of the members of the IRA's Army Council and, by phone, the US president, Bill Clinton. The prime minister's priority – to which he enlisted the taoiseach – was to rewrite strand two to keep the UUP leader on board. The result was a North/South Ministerial Council, the members of which, it was made clear, would operate 'in accordance with the rules for democratic authority and accountability in force in the Northern Ireland Assembly and the Oireachtas'. The long annexes were replaced with a list of 12 areas for possible co-operation, from which six 'implementation bodies' would be chosen by October 31st 1998. SDLP concerns that unionists might agree an assembly and then refuse to implement north-south co-operation were reflected in the provision that during the transition period before the actual transfer of powers to the new institutions, the six north-south schemes would be agreed.

Strand one

■ **O**n strand-two issues there had been a compromise between the SDLP and UUP, to the frustration of SF, which had stood out for a powerful north south institution, effectively independent of the Northern Ireland Assembly. On the negotiations about the assembly and executive, UUP acceptance of an SDLP model did not lessen republicans' difficulties with an institution which, until recently, they had denounced and refused to consider worthy of their participation.

The original UUP proposal had been for an administration operating on a system of executive committees, without ministers as such. Committee chairs would be distributed on a proportional basis according to the d'Hondt formula, as used in the European Parliament. The SDLP proposed a conventional executive with ministers and an elaborate range of checks and balances.

Concerned that the SDLP might be left open to attack by SF for alleged failure to look after the essential interests of nationalists – especially given the outcome on strand two – the UUP agreed to a full-blown ministerial system and to the SDLP's safeguard scheme. This was amended to limit the number of assembly decisions dependent on cross-communal majorities to a handful of circumstances, with a trigger mechanism that such a vote would be required for other matters if a 'petition of concern' was presented by 30 members.

The 'equality agenda', prisoners and decommissioning

■ **T**he focus of the UUP in the negotiations was on constitutional recognition and resisting any north-south body that could be realistically perceived as a staging post to a united Ireland. Satisfied that the agreement was in this sense 'structurally unionist', it paid much less attention to issues that could have major implications for the texture of life in Northern Ireland and create problems within the

Protestant community – being seen as legitimising a nationalist narrative about the history and structures of the northern state.

Thus in the section on 'Rights, Safeguards and Equality of Opportunity' one of the rights is 'to freedom from sectarian harassment' – which many republicans seek to apply directly to contested loyal-order marches. Similarly, in the section on 'Economic, Social and Cultural Issues' all participants 'acknowledge the sensitivity of the use of symbols and emblems for public purposes and the need ... to ensure that such symbols are used in a manner which promotes mutual respect'. This would provide the basis for SF ministers to claim that the agreement supported their decision that the Union flag would not be flown on their departmental buildings.

The decision to reduce, from three years to two, the timescale in which all prisoners belonging to paramilitary groups observing cease-fires would be released was, like UUP easy generosity on the 'equality agenda', seen as a means of shoring up an SF leadership that had effectively buried the republican project. Republican anger at the emerging UUP/SDLP centre of gravity, which had agreed strands one and two, was felt to need placating – whatever the problems this would create for pro-agreement unionists on such an emotive issue.

Similarly, the lack of a clear linkage between an IRA failure to decommission and the exclusion from office of SF ministers, with the latter dependent on a cross-community assembly vote – something most unionists believed the SDLP would never support – led to major problems on the last day of the negotiations. Urged by Mr Trimble and his main lieutenants to strengthen the procedures for exclusion, Mr Blair refused to alter the draft text. Instead, he provided the UUP leader with a letter promising that if, within the first six months of the operation of the shadow assembly or the assembly itself, the provisions on exclusion proved ineffective, he would support changes to them. With this fig-leaf, but having lost the support of Jeffrey Donaldson and some other members of his negotiating team, Mr Trimble agreed to sign up.

The next two years would see a gradual attrition of Protestant support for the agreement. Many came to focus not on its broad constitutional and political achievements for unionism, but on the more emotional issues of prisoner releases and SF ministers in power, with little sign of movement on decommissioning.

Bibliography

Mitchell, G (1999), Making Peace, London: Heinemann

6
Constitutional provisions
Tom Hadden

■ **T**he constitutional provisions of the agreement are the culmination of a painfully slow progression from confrontation between the UK and the Republic of Ireland on the status of Northern Ireland. The result has been the full acceptance of the principle of self-determination for its people and inter-state co-operation in the protection of the interests of both main religious communities.

Constitutional confrontation

■ **T**he confrontation on Northern Ireland's constitutional status stemmed from the denial by Irish republicans of the legitimacy of partition. This was reflected in the Free State constitution of 1937, which in article 2 asserted sovereignty over the whole island and then in article 3 withdrew it for all practical purposes. But the existence of the claim provided a formal basis for the campaign by the IRA and other militant republicans to end British rule in the 'six counties'.

When the south finally left the Commonwealth in 1948, the British government responded in the Ireland Act of 1949 by asserting jurisdiction over Northern Ireland and providing that no part of it could cease to be part of his majesty's dominions without the consent of a majority in the Northern Ireland Parliament. But it too continued to treat the Republic of Ireland as in practice less foreign than other countries, notably in respect of immigration.

The Sunningdale agreement

■ The first attempt to resolve the constitutional impasse came in the Sunningdale agreement of December 1973. But the two governments could not agree on a single formulation and resorted to parallel statements. London stated clearly that Northern Ireland was part of the UK. But Dublin said only that 'there could be no change in the status of Northern Ireland until a majority of the people of Northern Ireland desired a change in that status' – what that status might be was deliberately left undefined.

The political impact of the agreement was in any event immediately undermined by a legal challenge in the Irish courts in which it was held that the statement did not detract in any way from the constitutional claim (Boland v An Taoiseach 1974, Irish Reports 338). That decision, and the proposal for a new Council of Ireland, strengthened unionist opposition to the power-sharing government established in January 1974, brought down by a loyalist strike in May.

The Anglo-Irish Agreement

■ The Anglo-Irish Agreement of 1985 derived from negotiations following the report the previous year of the New Ireland Forum established by the republic's government. It was based on the principle of co-operation between London and Dublin and formal acceptance by the UK that the republic's government had a legitimate interest in the welfare of nationalists in Northern Ireland.

The agreement also included a joint, intergovernmental statement which went a little further towards formal recognition of the status of Northern Ireland. It said that any change in status would only come about with the consent of a majority of the people of Northern Ireland, and that the current wish of a majority was for no change.

That agreement was the subject of legal challenge too, this time in both Irish and British courts. The latter held they had no jurisdiction over what was essentially a political matter (ex parte Molyneaux 1986, 1 Weekly Law Reports 331). But the Supreme Court in the republic gave support to the popular view of its constitution held by both nationalists and unionists – ruling that reunification of the national territory was a 'constitutional imperative'. The court also held that the wording of the agreement did not infringe that obligation (McGimpsey v Ireland 1992, Irish Reports 110).

The Downing Street Declaration

■ It was not until the Downing Street Declaration of 1993 that Dublin felt able to commit itself to removal of the constitutional claim in the context of an overall political settlement. In exchange London affirmed it had no selfish or strategic interest in control of Northern Ireland, and reaffirmed that it would take any necessary action to achieve reunification if a majority voted for it.

Sustained efforts were made throughout 1995 in the Forum for Peace and Reconciliation established by the republic's government in the wake of the IRA cease-fire to persuade the republican movement to accept this formulation of the 'consent principle'. The IRA was unable to accept such a fundamental change in its approach to 'self-determination by the Irish people' and its cease-fire ended in February 1996. But the process of governmental and inter-party negotiation on an overall settlement continued.

The Belfast Agreement

■ **T**he constitutional provisions of the Belfast Agreement are an attempt to provide a more comprehensive and longer-term resolution of inter-related issues that are problematic in a territory shared by adherents of two national or ethnic identities. There are five significant elements:

- a careful formulation of the principle of self-determination designed to satisfy both republicans and unionists;
- development of the principles of proportionality and cross-community consent in respect of internal self-government;
- separation of the concept of national identity from that of national territory;
- formal provision for inter-state co-operation on Northern Ireland affairs; and
- provision for reciprocal guarantees in the event of a change of sovereignty over Northern Ireland.

(i)   The idea that the right of 'the Irish people as a whole' to determine their future was denied by partition has been a fundamental tenet of the republican movement since the 1920s. The concept of self-determination by the Irish nation was consequently given pride of place in article 1 of the 1937 constitution.

One of the main objectives of the settlement negotiations was to find a way of satisfying both the demand of republicans for an act of self-determination by the Irish people as a whole and the insistence of the British government and unionists that the consent of the people of Northern Ireland was required for any change in its status. The solution, originally proposed by the SDLP leader, John Hume, was to hold simultaneous referenda on the relevant aspects of a settlement north and south. This proposal was central to the Downing Street Declaration and its wording was incorporated into the Belfast Agreement:

It is for the people of the island of Ireland alone, by agreement between the two parts respectively and without external impediment, to exercise their right of self-determination on the basis of consent, freely and concurrently given, North and South, to bring about a united Ireland, if that is their wish, accepting that this right must be achieved and exercised with and subject to the agreement and consent of a majority of the people of Northern Ireland.

This formulation, together with a formal recognition of the legitimacy of the current wish of a majority of the people of Northern Ireland to be part of the UK, has been repeated in the new British-Irish Agreement, an international treaty signed by both governments. The right of the people of Northern Ireland to decide which state they shall belong to has been re-enacted in section 1 of the Northern Ireland Act 1998. And the claim to sovereignty over the whole island of Ireland in article 2 of the republic's constitution has been replaced by an aspiration to unity by consent in a new version of article 3:

It is the firm will of the Irish nation, in harmony and friendship, to unite all the people who share the territory of the island of Ireland, in all the diversity of their identities and traditions, recognising that a united Ireland shall be brought about only by peaceful means with the consent of a majority of the people, democratically expressed, in both jurisdictions in the island ...

(ii)   A somewhat different approach to self-determination has been adopted in respect of internal self-government in Northern Ireland. Unionists had typically sought to rely on majority rule, while nationalists had long complained about the 'unionist veto'. The resolution achieved in the negotiation of the Belfast Agreement was that the consent of representatives of both major communities was required for the government of a divided society. The provisions for the proportional allocation of executive positions and the registration of communal affiliation and cross-communal voting in the assembly attempt to give that practical effect.

The exercise of self-determination in internal government has thus been dealt with on an entirely different basis from the decision – a simple-majority vote – as to the state of which Northern Ireland is to be part. This is wholly in accord with the developing principles of international human-rights law on protection of minorities, which require states to provide for effective participation by members of 'national minorities' in the system of government.

(iii)   A further constitutional innovation is the clear separation of the concept of citizenship from that of national territory. The traditional concept of the nation-state is founded on the view that a 'nation' is entitled to a national territory and citizenship is based on birth in a state. These concepts were built into the 1937 constitution and it was a cause of concern to nationalists that recognition of the legitimacy of Northern Ireland as part of the UK might deprive them of their right to be Irish. The agreement and the new British-Irish Agreement deal with this by providing that all the people of Northern Ireland have the right to identify themselves and to be accepted as Irish or British or both, and that this right is not to be affected by any future change in the status of Northern Ireland.

This is reflected from a purely Irish perspective in the new version of article 2 of the constitution, which extends membership of the Irish nation to every person born in the island of Ireland and recognises the special affinity of the Irish nation with people of Irish ancestry living abroad. The idea of an Irish nation has thus been retained; the precise effect of membership of or affinity with the Irish nation, however, is not specified and may in due course require clarification.

(iv)   The Anglo-Irish Agreement initiated formal inter-state co-operation between London and Dublin on Northern Ireland. The procedures for consultation centred on issues relevant to the nationalist minority. It made a clear distinction between such consultation and joint authority, specifying that each government retained exclusive sovereignty within its jurisdiction. But the 1985 agreement was regarded by unionists as illegitimate interference in the internal affairs of the UK by a 'foreign' government, and they demanded that it should be replaced.

In this respect, however, the provisions of the Belfast Agreement are broadly similar. Consultation on the interests of northern nationalists has been replaced by a more general obligation to consult on all matters of mutual interest, but the special concern of the republic's government on Northern Ireland is explicitly recognised. As was anticipated in 1985, the obligation to consult excludes all matters on which power has been devolved to the assembly. The specific reference to the continuing sovereignty of each government within its jurisdiction has been retained. These provisions are supplemented by the new arrangements – wider but less specific – embodied in the British-Irish Council.

(v) The agreement also breaks new constitutional ground by committing both governments to guarantee the same rights and maintain the same respect for the diverse identities in Northern Ireland in the event of a change in sovereignty. The intention of this is to diminish the concerns of unionists, should nationalists become a majority in Northern Ireland, that their rights would be ignored within a unified Irish state.

One possible interpretation is that the complex arrangements for power-sharing in regional government should be continued even if a majority in Northern Ireland voted to leave the UK and join the republic. That would be consistent with the principles of an agreement designed to provide stability in a divided society by guaranteeing proportional participation in government regardless of the precise balance between the two main communities. But it is not yet clear whether the implications of this are fully understood or accepted by republicans, who regard the agreement as a stepping stone to a unitary, sovereign Irish state.

It would be unwise to attempt at this early stage to dictate future developments. But the reciprocal governmental guarantees should at least help to reduce the potential for future conflict as the balance between the two main communities in Northern Ireland becomes more equal.

the Belfast Agreement

7

The Assembly

Rick Wilford

The consociational bargain

■ **T**he intricacy of the Belfast Agreement is nowhere more apparent than in its interlocking architecture, erected on the foundations of earlier, ill-fated, attempts to restore devolved government to Northern Ireland following the imposition of direct rule in 1972. Indeed, a wry observation by Séamus Mallon, deputy leader of the SDLP and now deputy first minister, gives a clue to its antecedents: 'Sunningdale for slow learners'.

The 1998 agreement, like the failed 1973-74 arrangements, represents an exercise in consociational democracy (Wilford, 1992, 1999; O'Leary, 1999): the new institutions are based upon principles deemed necessary where the wider social and political context is inimical to majoritarianism, as is typical of deeply divided societies. The characteristics of consociational democracies are designed to accommodate the interests, needs and, more negatively, mutual suspicion harboured by political rivals. Indeed, Arend Lijphart (1968, 1969), the progenitor of consociationalism, captured the essence of this model of democratic government in the term 'the politics of accommodation' – a phrase often deployed by the signatories of the Belfast Agreement as a riposte to those who represent it as an appeasement.

One such accommodative characteristic is power-sharing, a shorthand term for consociationalism. This prescribes the need for coalition government among the contending parties. Power-sharing is present in 'strand one' of the agreement in three ways: the 12-member, four-party coalition comprising the Executive Committee; the relationship between the executive and the assembly; and the intra-assembly relations among the parties, notably within the statutory committees. The agreement, and the Northern Ireland Act 1998 which gives it legislative effect, describe a partnership within and between the executive and legislature consistent with consociational principles.

The second feature of consociationalism is proportionality, including in electoral systems, allocation of public expenditure and public employment. Underpinning its application are notions of fairness and social justice, the principle that no one sector of society will benefit from any disproportionate distribution of public goods. The principle is perhaps most obviously apparent in the method of electing representatives to the assembly, the single transferable vote, a form of proportional representation familiar to the region's electorate. Proportionality also extends to the composition of the assembly's committees and to the allocation of their chairs and deputy chairs who, like the members of the executive, are appointed by application of the d'Hondt rule, named after its Belgian inventor, Viktor d'Hondt[1] (see chapter 8).

The third characteristic of a consociation is segmental autonomy, which translates into the maxim 'high fences make good neighbours'. This enables communities to enjoy autonomy over matters of central concern to their sense of identity (religious, ethnic, national, cultural or linguistic). In effect, it endorses social segregation. While the agreement is not consistent on this – supporting integrated education while endorsing the mainly segregated schooling system – its underlying bi-national character, giving equal legitimacy to 'British' and 'Irish' cultural identities, is interpreted in 'separate but equal' terms.

The final aspect of consociations is a mutual veto among political élites – in practice, a unanimity rule among decision-makers. This applies within the executive on what the agreement defines as 'key decisions', including the Programme for Government and budget allocations. (The unanimity rule also applies to the North/South Ministerial Council in 'strand two'.) Such decisions also require cross-community consent within the assembly.

The results

■ **T**he agreement envisaged an 108-member assembly based on Northern Ireland's 18 Westminster constituencies, each returning six members. The referendum a month later recorded a 'yes' vote of 71 per cent,[2] and the assembly election in June 1998 saw pro-agreement candidates secure 73 per cent of first-preference votes – which translated into 80 seats for the pro-agreement parties and 28 for those opposed.[3] But that overwhelming majority in favour of the consociational bargain could not disguise the sharp division among unionist supporters.[4]

The unionist electorate's ambivalence about the agreement was thrown into sharp relief by the UUP's 21.3 per cent first-preference tally. This was its worst ever performance in an STV election, left it just three points clear of the DUP (18 per cent), and meant that for the first time in Northern Ireland's history, a nationalist party, the SDLP, topped the poll (22 per cent). With SF scoring 17.7 per cent, the nationalist bloc's aggregate performance was its best ever in a PR election, although the outworking of the electorate's preferences rewarded the UUP with a seat bonus such that it emerged as the single largest party in the assembly.[5]

The acuteness of unionist division was underlined on the first day of the 'shadow' assembly, July 1st. Members were obliged by the agreement (and the act) to register as 'unionist', 'nationalist' or 'other' as they signed the roll, so that votes on 'key decisions' – which require cross-community consent – could be effected. The registration confirmed that there were 30 pro-agreement unionists in the assembly and 28 opposed. Worse for David Trimble, a number of UUP members were known to have voted 'no' and, on the matter of SF's participation in government, would prove awkward allies of the party leader. Indeed, one, Peter Weir, subsequently resigned the party whip to sit with the DUP, thereby creating an exact split within the unionist bloc.

The 'shadow' assembly

■ **U**ntil the transfer of devolved powers on December 2nd 1999,[6] the assembly lingered long in shadow. Also on day one came the election of Messrs Trimble and Mallon as, respectively, first and deputy first minister (designate). Required by the agreement to run for office jointly, this was an eloquent expression of power-sharing since, while their titles differ, they are co-equals under the agreement and the act.

During the shadow phase the assembly's members were preoccupied largely with the standing orders. Drafting was delegated to an all-party committee, which was jointly chaired by a unionist and a nationalist member, again epitomising the power-sharing principle emblematic of consociation, as did its inclusive membership. The endorsement of standing orders, in the committee and the assembly as a whole, had to be cross-community, being – like the election of the FM and DFM and budgetary allocations – a 'key decision'.

All key decisions have to surmount one of two tests: 'parallel consent' or 'weighted majority'. The former requires an overall majority, including a majority of both self-designated unionists and nationalists; the latter requires 60 per cent of members, including at least 40 per cent of both unionists and nationalists. Both safeguard against majoritarianism on strategic issues, as does the agreement's provision for a 'petition of concern': 30 assembly members can seek to designate any issue as a key decision.

Between July and December 1998, while negotiations continued over draft standing orders, events beyond the assembly had a decisive effect. The agreement stipulated that the committees of the assembly – membership of which would broadly reflect party strengths – were to operate in tandem with the devolved departments. But it was not until December 18th 1998 that the number of departments was agreed, after protracted negotiations between, for the most part, the two larger parties, the UUP and SDLP. In addition to the office to service the Trimble and Mallon dyarchy, the negotiators agreed to create ten new departments. This meant there would be 12 ministers in all in the executive: six unionists and six nationalists.

The four-party executive included three pro-agreement parties – UUP, SDLP and SF – and one, the DUP, unequivocally opposed. This meant that there was no formal (let alone, 'loyal') 'opposition' within the assembly, unlike its counterparts in Cardiff and Edinburgh, or indeed Westminster. However, while there was no opposition team, in the sense of a 'government-in-waiting', the role of challenging the executive was to an extent ascribed to the statutory committees.

The agreement specified that the statutory committees would scrutinise their associated departments, assist in the development of policy and be able to initiate legislation. They were thus intended to be powerful, multi-functional bodies with consensual working arrangements, establishing a nexus between the executive and the assembly in policy and legislative matters.

The assembly, in plenary, is the prime source of legislative authority on devolved matters. Thus, while a minister, the executive as a whole, an individual member or a statutory committee may propose legislation, the assembly disposes. While all key decisions have to secure cross-community support, all others are subject to simple majority. This enables speedier handling of some business and allows individual members to exercise some autonomy from the party fold.

In addition to the statutory committees, the standing orders committee recommended a range of standing committees. Common to parliamentary systems, these included standards and privileges, audit, procedures, public accounts and a business committee. With the exception of the five-strong audit committee, all were to have 11 members, like the statutory committees, with the same d'Hondt-derived allocation of chair and vice-chair positions.

The legislative role of the assembly is constrained. Besides being limited to transferred matters and with the special voting procedures for key decisions, any legislation must comply with the European Convention on Human Rights and any Northern Ireland Bill of Rights that may supplement it. Also, all legislation and policy must be 'equality-proofed': it must comply with the statutory obligation to promote equality of opportunity as well as 'parity of esteem' between the two dominant communities. These tests, overseen by two new extra-governmental bodies, the Northern Ireland Human Rights Commission and the multi-purpose Equality Commission, provide further safeguards against any abuse of power.

Devolution: phase one

∎ **T**he long shadow period extended almost throughout 1999, due to the impasse over decommissioning of paramilitary weapons. In November, following an 11-week review of the implementation of the agreement chaired by the talks chair, George Mitchell – triggered by the resignation of Mr Mallon as DFM the previous July amid the failure to nominate an inclusive executive – Mr Trimble sought the endorsement of his party's governing Ulster Unionist Council to enter devolved government alongside the three other major parties. This secured, the assembly convened on November 29th to facilitate the nominations of executive members and the chairs and deputy chairs of the statutory committees. Three days later, following the passage of the devolution order in the Commons, powers were transferred – almost 20 months after the Belfast Agreement was reached.

The initial phase of devolution, which lasted 72 days until its suspension by the Northern Ireland secretary, Peter Mandelson, on February 11th 2000, said much about relationships between the devolved departments and the statutory committees. Although intended as transparent partnerships, the committees – unlike those in the Welsh National Assembly and the Scottish Parliament – began by engaging in mostly private meetings with ministers, officials and other interests to set their agendas. Given the delay in devolving powers, neither the committees nor the assembly as a whole were in a position properly to scrutinise the expenditure allocations announced in December 1999 by the new finance minister, Mark Durkan (themselves inherited from the direct-rule administration).[7]

Moreover, little progress was consequently made on the Programme for Government, intended to be a collaborative venture between the executive and the assembly, structured through the committees. Thus, while the institutions of each of the agreement's three 'strands' were swiftly put in place and budgetary allocations made, the impact of the assembly was tangential.

Two issues raised widespread concern among members about the effectiveness of the relationships between ministers and the committees. The Department of Health, Social Services and Public Safety, and its statutory committee, were faced with the long-simmering matter of the location of maternity services in Belfast. The choice for the new minister, Bairbre de Brún, lay between the City

Hospital, in south Belfast, and the Royal Victoria Hospital, a mile away in her west Belfast constituency. She opted for the latter, whereas the committee had voted by a 7-4 majority in favour of the City, a view echoed later by the assembly (voting largely along sectarian lines).[8] Ms de Brún's decision was taken under existing ministerial authority and thereby did not require new legislation, or even the consent of her ministerial colleagues. The only recourse available to those opposed to her decision was to seek a judicial review. As a test of assembly/executive power-sharing, this episode was a failure.

The other matter concerned the accountability of the Office of the First and Deputy First Minister. The assembly's standing orders committee originally proposed one committee to scrutinise the OFMDFM on equality matters, one of the functions allocated to the office.[9] But the committee was not satisfied with this partial accountability and revisited the issue in December 1999, securing assembly support for a plan for two standing committees to scrutinise a wider range of functions: equality, human rights and community relations; and European affairs.[10] On December 14th, an attempt was made to create a third committee, to examine and report on the remaining functions of the office (which total 26), but this was countered by an amendment from the FM and the DFM.

They sought instead to replace the two committees by a single 'committee of the centre', responsible for scrutinising around half of the office's responsibilities – in effect excluding from its remit all matters relating to the north-south and British-Irish dimensions of the agreement.[11] With UUP and SDLP members voting en bloc, the amendment was passed. Where there were to be two, and potentially three, committees to scrutinise the OFMDFM, now there was to be one, much to the disquiet of members from all other parties. Such heavy-handedness by Messrs Trimble and Mallon disclosed what many in the assembly had suspected – that, acting in concert, the UUP and the SDLP were virtually an irresistible force.

If anything, the suspicion was confirmed when the FM and DFM tabled a joint determination to appoint two junior ministers to their office, a proposal subject to a simple-majority vote.[12] Again acting in unison, the two parties endorsed the determination and on December 15th the appointments were duly made: one UUP (Dermot Nesbitt), the other SDLP (Denis Haughey). The appointments underlined the view that the OFMDFM was a closed shop for the two major parties.

Devolution: phase two

■ **T**he suspension meant that the assembly, along with the other new institutions, suffered a period of arrested development. The return of devolution on May 29th left the statutory committees with no alternative but to reacquaint themselves with developments in their departments – thereby occasioning more delay in the production of their work plans. Moreover, the timing of the UK government's budget in March again prevented the proper scrutiny of consequent expenditure allocations. In addition, the executive and the assembly had had little opportunity to contribute to the Comprehensive Spending Review whose results were announced in July, setting out plans for 2001-04.

The assembly was, in effect, playing 'catch-up' during this second phase, and by July 4th it was into a two-month summer recess. The faltering implementation of devolution also meant that work by the executive on the Programme for Government, which had to be agreed unanimously by ministers and secure cross-community consent in the assembly, was delayed.

There were, however, febrile debates on symbolic and constitutional issues. In the light of the refusal of SF ministers to countenance the flying of the Union flag over their departments, on June 6th the DUP moved a 'petition of concern' that 'this assembly directs that the Union flag should be flown on executive buildings in NI on all designated days, in keeping with the arrangements of other parts of the UK and, additionally, on Parliament Buildings on all sitting days.' The vote was 53 in favour, 41 against, but it failed because it lacked the necessary cross-community support.

At the party's third attempt, on the last day of the session, the DUP secured the 30 signatures required to move a petition seeking to exclude SF from ministerial office entirely, as allegedly not committed to exclusively peaceful and democratic means.[13] A UUP member, Pauline Armitage, dissatisfied with the terms of the deal on decommissioning worked out by the parties and the governments in early May, had added her name to the petition. This forced a vote on July 4th, in which two other UUP members, Roy Beggs Jnr and Derek Hussey, voted with the DUP and other anti-agreement unionists.

While the vote was lost because it again did not attract the required cross-community support, it did reveal that pro-agreement unionists were now in the minority (26 to 32) in the unionist bloc on the matter of SF's continuing participation in government. The DUP's success in mustering sufficient support to trigger a debate and a vote suggests that the petition device will be further employed – in a manner designed to cause maximum embarrassment to the UUP in general and Mr Trimble in particular.

Conclusion

■ **F**ar from being in advance of Scotland and Wales, as originally envisaged, Northern Ireland now lags some way behind in the devolution process. Any judgment of its progress at this stage must be heavily qualified. The 'strand one' institutions have only begun to find their feet and to develop a set of working relationships – and these, to date, have not realised the partnership envisaged in the agreement.

During the shadow period and the two phases of devolution, the parties have mostly worked together. But the assembly was, at this writing, just getting to grips with a legislative programme, home-grown budgetary proposals and procedures, and subjecting the devolved departments to full scrutiny. In these key respects, the test of the new consociational arrangements could not be said to have been met.

Inter-party relationships within the assembly – especially between pro- and anti-agreement unionists, and between the latter and SF – have been sorely and increasingly strained. One symptom was the decision of four members of the UUP to vote for the exclusion of SF from the Executive Committee in the debate on the DUP's petition of concern.

On the credit side, the assembly engaged in a number of debates – including abortion, equality, expenditure allocations, hospital closures, the Patten report on policing, flags and transport. It also made provision for ministerial question time on Mondays, when three ministers appear in succession for 30 minutes each to answer oral questions. The committees continued to operate, although still in their infancy and yet to exert a decisive effect on their departments and associated bodies. The assembly embarked on an initial legislative programme, but this was partly governed by the desire to maintain parity with developments at Westminster.[14] While it had some opportunity to debate expenditure allocations this was limited, especially in relation to the appropriation debate shortly after the restoration of devolution.

While the principle of proportionality has been applied successfully to the assembly's committees, that of partnership between the assembly and the executive has as yet failed to develop. Perhaps the most benign measure of the assembly's performance is that to date it has survived, if not entirely unscathed.

Bibliography

Hadfield, B (1998), 'The Belfast Agreement, sovereignty and the state of the union', Public Law, 599-616

– – – (1999), 'The nature of devolution to Scotland and Northern Ireland: key issues of responsibility and control', Edinburgh Law Review, 3, 3-31

Lijphart, A (1968), The Politics of Accommodation: Pluralism and Democracy in the Netherlands, Berkeley and Los Angeles: University of California Press

– – – (1969), 'Consociational Democracy', World Politics, 21, 207-225

O'Leary, B (1999), 'The nature of the British-Irish agreement', New Left Review, 233, 66-96

Wilford, R (1992), 'Inverting consociationalism? policy, pluralism and the post-modern', in Hadfield, B (ed), Northern Ireland: Politics and the Constitution, Buckingham: Open University Press, 29-48

– – – (1999), 'Epilogue', in Mitchell, P and Wilford, R (eds), Politics in Northern Ireland, Boulder, Co: Westview Press, 285-304

Notes to the text

[1] The d'Hondt rule does not tend to deliver strict proportionality: it favours larger parties in most circumstances. The UUP and SDLP secured 60 per cent of executive seats, based on 48 per cent of assembly seats and an even lower proportion (43.3 per cent) of first-preference votes.

[2] The simultaneous referendum in the republic produced a turnout of 56.3 per cent and an emphatic vote in favour of the agreement and the consequential changes to articles 2 and 3 of the 1937 constitution: 94.4 per cent voted in favour. The combined 'yes' vote on the island was almost 83 per cent.

[3] The 80 seats comprised 28 UUP, 24 SDLP, 18 SF, 6 Alliance Party, 2 Progressive Unionists and 2 Women's Coalition. The anti-agreement bloc consisted of 20 DUP, 5 UK Unionists and 3 Independent Unionists. The latter three later joined forces under the United Unionist Assembly Party, while four members of the UKUP broke away to form the Northern Ireland Unionist Party.

[4] Two referendum exit polls in Northern Ireland showed that a narrow majority of unionist electors had voted in favour of the agreement (Sunday Times, May 24th 1998; RTE, May 23rd 1998).

[5] The 'seat bonus' is calculated by subtracting from the proportion of assembly seats won by a party the proportion of its first-preference vote. The UUP, which won 25.9 per cent of seats, did so on 21.3 per cent of first preferences, thereby achieving a

bonus of 4.6 per cent. The SDLP experienced a seat bonus of 0.2 per cent and the DUP of 0.4 per cent, whereas both SF and Alliance experienced a discrepancy of ñ0.9 per cent between their vote share and proportion of seats won.

[6] The transferred powers are those formerly exercised by the six departments that existed under direct rule (Hadfield 1998, 1999).

[7] Northern Ireland Assembly Report (hereafter NIAR), December 15th 1999

[8] NIAR, January 31st 2000

[9] The statement on the allocation of functions was made during the shadow period. See New Northern Ireland Assembly Report, February 15th 1999. Note that the prefix 'New' was dropped from the title of the official report after the transfer of devolved powers in December 1999.

[10] NIAR, December 6th 1999

[11] NIAR, December 14th 1999

[12] ibid

[13] NIAR, July 4th 2000

[14] NIAR, January 31st 2000. The initial legislative programme announced by the first minister included, besides the first Appropriation Bill: the Equality (Disability etc) Bill; the Child Support, Pensions and Social Security Bill; the Trustees (Amendment) Bill; the Ground Rents Bill; the Deregulation (Weights and Measures) Bill; the Dogs Bill, which was to amend the Dogs (NI) Order 1983; and the Fisheries (Amendment) Bill. Short explanations of the purposes of each bill were included in the FM's statement.

8

The Executive Committee

Robin Wilson

Government by numbers

■ If the nature of direct rule in Northern Ireland was to leave everyone in opposition, the nature of the Belfast Agreement was to put everyone (all significant parties, at least) into government – a remarkable transition.

Within a week of their election, the 108 members of the assembly met on July 1st 1998 to elect the first and deputy first minister. The agreement provided for 'key decisions' to require 'parallel consent' or a 'weighted majority' (see chapter 7). The election of the FM and DFM, the Northern Ireland Act 1998 stipulated, could only be by the first procedure, and both had to be elected together.

The UUP leader, Mr Trimble, and the SDLP deputy leader, Mr Mallon, were duly elected, respectively as FM and DFM, because the UUP enjoyed a greater 'seat bonus' in the assembly election than the stronger-polling SDLP. (The SDLP leader, John Hume, finally decided on the day of the vote that he would not go forward for election as DFM.)

The agreement established that the remainder of the Executive Committee would be formed by the d'Hondt mechanism, rather than by agreement between parties. The process involves the iterative operation of the formula $x = y/(1+z)$, where y = the number of assembly seats held by a party after the last election and z = the number of positions allocated to it. At each point the party for which x is the largest number is allocated a position of its choice from those remaining. (If there is a tie at any point, y is redefined as the number of first-preference votes for the party at the last election.)

After prolonged negotiations in late 1998 over the number of departments, the UUP acceded in December to the demand of the SDLP that there be 10 ministerial offices, as against the six prevailing Northern Ireland departments (New Northern Ireland Assembly Report 7, February 15th 1999). The unspoken calculus was that SF would not be satisfied with only one executive seat; ten departments were required to ensure the party enjoyed two. The result was an allocation of ministerial positions as follows: SF two, SDLP three, UUP three and DUP two.

An abortive attempt was made by the Northern Ireland secretary, Marjorie Mowlam, to run the d'Hondt rule in July 1999, after further inconclusive discussions on decommissioning, but a unionist boycott nullified the procedure. Finally, in the wake of the (apparently) successful review of the implementation of the agreement by George Mitchell, the process was conducted in the assembly at the end of November that year.

Executive decision

∎ **A** decision by the UUP to secure the cultural ministry before SF could claim it (given the sensitivity of identity issues) allowed SF to secure the education portfolio; when the latter party later took health it found itself in command of the two big spending departments. Also notable was that the parties only nominated two women for ministerial positions, and that they were allocated the last two choices of department (health and agriculture).

Including the FM and DFM, this meant the composition of the Executive Committee was as follows:

- David Trimble (UUP): first minister
- Seámus Mallon (SDLP): deputy first minister
- Reg Empey (UUP): minister of enterprise, trade and investment
- Mark Durkan (SDLP): minister of finance and personnel
- Peter Robinson (DUP): minister for regional development
- Martin McGuinness (SF): minister of education
- Sam Foster (UUP): minister of environment
- Sean Farren (SDLP): minister of higher and further education, training and employment
- Nigel Dodds (DUP): minister for social development
- Michael McGimpsey (UUP): minister of culture, arts and leisure
- Bairbre de Brún (SF): minister of health, social services and public safety
- Bríd Rodgers (SDLP): minister of agriculture and rural development

The suspension of the executive in mid-February 2000, due to the unravelling of the Mitchell review, led to a further hiatus before the executive was re-established, on foot of new IRA commitments, at the end of May. The new policy of rotating ministers adopted by the DUP meant Messrs Robinson and Dodds were replaced by Gregory Campbell and Maurice Morrow respectively at the end of July.

Swiss roles

■ **N**owhere else in the world is government formed by the d'Hondt rule, whose more normal role is the allocation of top-up seats under additional-member systems of proportional representation. It arose in the agreement because of a compromise in the days leading up to Good Friday 1998 between the UUP proposal of administrative devolution, with committee chairs allocated by d'Hondt, and the SDLP demand for power-sharing, cabinet government. Rather like the camel that emerged from the committee designing a horse, a power-sharing executive with positions distributed by d'Hondt was the outcome.

The Swiss 'magic formula' for allocation of the seven seats in the Federal Council is the nearest any other jurisdiction comes to such a mechanistic process of government formation. Even there, there are two crucial contrasts.

First, the decentralisation of power in Switzerland – lying largely with the 26 cantons and more than 3,000 communes – and the option of referenda to contest government decisions provide checks and balances against the danger that an executive with no real opposition will become unaccountable. Secondly, in Switzerland the whole parliament gets to vote for the seven council members – they are not simply party appointees. Thus elected representatives on the left have a say in who represents the right, and vice versa, which obviously favours a spirit of reciprocity. In that sense, Switzerland is not simply an instance of the 'consociational' model of separate 'pillars', dominated by political élites, on which Northern Ireland's arrangements are premised. It is, rather, a grassroots, consensus democracy – if one not without its problems (ECMI, nd).

Belgium does have a formula also at the federal level, where government is formed equally by representatives of the Flemings and Walloons (Fitzmaurice, 1998) – a simple enough matter since the parties are each divided into separate wings by language-group. But, unlike in Northern Ireland, the principle of equality has been distinguished from that of inclusiveness: there is no requirement that all parties be in government and, indeed, the current centre-left administration leaves out the large Christian Democrat group, which had been in a succession of previous cabinets.

Top-down, and divided

■ The implication of these comparisons is clear and explains the two big difficulties which have beset the Northern Ireland devolved administration. First, looked at vertically, it is very élite-dominated – a continuation of the political style of the 'peace process' but likely to lead to real stresses. One has only to look at the bad feeling created by the health minister's overriding of her committee's majority view on the location of maternity services in Belfast in January 1999 – and the failure to explain her decision to the committee in the first instance – to see the pitfalls that the exercise of executive authority in this context can engender. The fundamental problem is that the requirement for inclusiveness means it is impossible for voters to achieve the most elemental result of democratic elections: to 'turf the scoundrels out'.

Secondly, looked at horizontally, it contains none of the ideological 'cement' which ensures the cohesion of coalitions between like-minded parties. As has been frequently remarked, devolution signalled in Northern Ireland a four-party, involuntary coalition. To hold that together would be difficult enough in any circumstances, with the obvious temptations – particularly approaching elections – for parties to trumpet the work of their ministries and to suggest that only the obstacles placed in their way by others prevented even more heroic achievements. But there is more than that.

In as much as the agreement institutionalised the unionist-nationalist conflict, rather than developed a new, multi-cultural, constitutional option, it did not hold out any new concept of Northern Ireland as a *sui generis* entity to which all its citizens could give allegiance. In the absence of any such regional alignment – an absence symbolised by the continued intimidating presence in front of Stormont of the statue of Lord Carson, rather than, say, a sculpture of the regionalist poet John Hewitt – parties have no overarching way of identifying a larger 'common good'. Yet this is crucial if they are to feel any obligation to subordinate partisan agendas to the public interest, and if the SDLP and UUP in particular are to be able to legitimise compromise to their supporters without fearing ethnic outbidding by their rivals.

At the end of the day, the Executive Committee, even if there is an automaticity about its formation, is a voluntary coalition in the more limited sense that parties can decline to continue to participate, and the smaller pair (DUP, SF) may *in extremis* be excluded by their partners. Were this to be the fate of the DUP, their seats could be redistributed under d'Hondt (to the UUP and Alliance in current circumstances) and the world would not fall in. The unspoken, but very real, understanding is that were it to be the fate of SF the IRA cease-fire would end. The proximate threat lies in the potential departure of the UUP, were Mr Trimble's now wafer-thin majority in his party to be overturned. In that case, the agreement would be finished.

Bibliography

European Centre for Minority Issues, 'Switzerland: an overlooked case of Europeanization?', undated paper, Flensburg: ECMI

Fitzmaurice, J (1998), 'Diversity and civil society', in Wilson, R ed, New Order? International Models of Peace and Reconciliation, Belfast: Democratic Dialogue, pp 49-65

9

The Civic Forum

John Woods

Introduction

■ The Civic Forum arising from the Belfast Agreement introduces an innovative and exciting element to the governance of Northern Ireland. Although viewed with some scepticism by many elected representatives, the potential of the forum lies in bringing the resources and goodwill of civil society to bear in support of the work of the assembly.

The concept of a civic forum was introduced to the negotiations leading to the agreement by the Women's Coalition. Rooted in civil society rather than in traditional politics, the coalition wanted to ensure that a civil-society contribution was officially recognised as part of the new political dispensation.

What emerged from the negotiations was a single paragraph in the agreement:

A consultative Civic Forum will be established. It will comprise representatives of the business, trade union and voluntary

sectors, and such other sectors as agreed by the First Minister
and Deputy First Minister. It will act as a consultative mechanism
on social, economic and cultural issues. The First Minister and
Deputy First Minister will by agreement provide administrative
support for the Civic Forum and establish guidelines for the
selection of representatives to the Civic Forum.

This set the stage for considerable interest from the sectors named,
as well as farming organisations and the churches in particular.
Although no official consultative process was established, in
subsequent months the first and deputy first ministers designate
received submissions from a variety of organisations expressing their
interest in the forum and offering suggestions as to its role, remit and
composition.

The first and deputy first ministers' proposals

■ In February 1999 the FM and DFM placed their proposals for
the Civic Forum before the assembly (New Northern Ireland
Assembly Report 7, February 15th 1999). The report reiterated the
words of the agreement, describing the role of the forum as 'a
consultative mechanism on social, economic and cultural issues'. The
ministers said they would 'make arrangements for obtaining from the
Civic Forum its views on such matters'. The remainder of the report
was devoted to its composition.

Thus the forum would comprise 60 members plus a chairperson
nominated for three-year terms as follows:

business	7
agriculture/fisheries	3
trade union	7
voluntary/community	18*
churches	5

culture	4
arts and sport	4
victims	2
community relations	2
education	2
first and deputy first ministers	6

* The voluntary/community sector is divided into 11 sub-sectors: older people, youth, people with disabilities, women's groups, ethnic minorities, carers, families and children, community development, community health, community education and environmental groups.

All nominating bodies (organisations and consortia of organisations within each sector) were required to achieve 'a gender balance; a community background balance; a geographic spread across Northern Ireland; and a balanced age profile to include young people and older people'. They were also required to 'adhere to the principles of public appointments being based on equality of opportunity, merit, openness and transparency of process'.

A chair was appointed by the FM and DFM 'following a process of consultation and public advertisement'. He is Chris Gibson, a Northern Ireland business leader.

In practical terms it is expected that there will be approximately six plenary sessions of the forum each year, with most work being done in working groups. Members are likely to have to spend 2-4 days a month on forum business. There will be a review of the structure and operation of the forum within 12 months of its establishment.

Many would view the composition of the forum as imperfect. It appears to attempt to include all sections of society – an impossible task which only serves to draw attention to the fact that many interests have not been included. The forum is dominated by the voluntary/community sectors: the traditional social partners have fewer seats between them. There is a grave danger that business and the trade unions will look elsewhere for their primary engagement with government.

Ways of overcoming these problems include ensuring that the
forum takes account of all views, rather than containing all views
within it, and that forum members act as servants of wider society
rather than guardians of sectional interests. The vital connection and
interaction with wider society could be achieved through innovative
forms of participation and public involvement.

Debates about the forum

■ **T**he above proposals concentrate almost exclusively on who is in
the forum and how they are appointed. Some clues as to what the
forum is actually for are to be found in the debates which have taken
place among civil-society organisations and politicians since the
proposal first saw the light of day.

Much of the debate on the nature and role of the forum has been
informed by the notion of governance, in reaction to the failure of
traditional forms of government to deliver on public expectations.
Administrations can no longer pull simple macro-economic levers to
secure full employment, for example; public-spending constraints
mean a constantly dissatisfied electorate; and trans-national
companies operate to their own set of rules. The concept of
governance recognises these constraints and seeks to achieve policy
goals by utilising the knowledge and skills in wider society through a
wide range of partnerships and networks. Clearly the Civic Forum has
the potential to nurture the effective governance of Northern Ireland,
through marrying the skills and knowledge of the sectors it represents
with those of elected representatives, public administration and the
wider society.

Considerable consensus has been built up within civil society (New
Agenda, 1998; Democratic Dialogue, 1999) on how the forum can
most effectively contribute to politics in Northern Ireland. One
suggestion was that it should comment on all or selected assembly

legislation, a task which would certainly keep it extremely busy. It would also be likely to be of limited value, given that the forum would lack any powers of amendment and would be entering the process of policy development at a very late stage.

It has also been suggested that the forum should respond to specific requests from the assembly to work on particular issues, and that it should be able to initiate work of its own. The strengths of the forum could be utilised in this regard, drawing on its capacity to take a holistic perspective and to produce a seamless narrative on multifaceted problems. It could use its capacity to be innovative and creative to best effect and could carefully consider its role in tackling division in Northern Ireland. On one view, the forum is nothing if it has not the courage to confront issues like 'punishment' beatings and parading, even if these areas do not fall within the remit of the assembly. Arguably, the forum would find it easier than the assembly to deal with them.

In social, economic and cultural policy, the forum can play best to its strengths by working in areas which cut across the traditional departments of government – the so-called 'wicked issues'. Examples could include addressing long-term unemployment, pursuing sustainable development, tackling crime or applying a broader focus to the delivery and monitoring of economic strategy.

Another area of activity in which the forum could make a vital contribution is in the iterative reformulation of the Programme for Government. If the programme is going to depend on the co-operation of the social partners and a range of social actors for its delivery, the involvement of the forum is likely to enhance the government's ability to deliver on public expectations. Similarly, the participation of the forum in the budgeting process would strengthen the outcome of that process.

A unique political contribution

■ **W**hatever the forum decides, or is decided for it, its value and success will depend on setting the agenda in challenging policy areas – taking a long-term view and presenting a different kind of discourse. One senior politician has expressed the hope that the Civic Forum will challenge the assembly. The nature of four-party coalition government may, he fears, take consensus too far and there may be a danger of reducing policy to a lowest common denominator – the Civic Forum could be an important foil to such a tendency.

The value and success of the forum will also depend on rising to the challenge of doing something different, and going well beyond commenting on proposals drawn up by others. Offering opinions is not participation in governance. Rather, offering solutions to problems, together with a commitment to help deliver those solutions, is what ministers should reasonably expect in return for putting their faith in a Civic Forum.

Bibliography

New Agenda (1998), The Civic Forum: A Consultation Document, Belfast: New Agenda

Democratic Dialogue (1999), The Civic Forum and Negotiated Governance, Belfast: DD

10

North-south co-ordination
John Coakley

■ **T**he north-south relationship ('strand two') which the Belfast Agreement sought to institutionalise proceeded in subsequent years through the same hesitant steps as the other post-agreement institutions: a false start was followed by a fresh beginning. The agreement represents the third systematic effort since the partition of Ireland in 1921 to promote institutionalised co-operation. The first two, in 1925 and 1974, foundered on the rocks of nationalist indifference and unionist intransigence, respectively.

The Government of Ireland Act 1920 provided for a 41-member Council of Ireland, comprising an independent chair and 20 representatives each from the northern and southern parliaments. There was to be an all-Irish executive including the lord lieutenant, the lord chancellor and the Privy Council of Ireland. Transferred civil servants and others appointed by the council would service its needs. It would be responsible initially for private bills, railways, fisheries and infectious diseases of animals. Powers that might later be transferred included responsibility for the Post Office, for the registration of deeds and the Public Record Office.

The Sunningdale agreement of 1973 provided for a 60-member Consultative Assembly, comprising 30 representatives each from the northern and southern parliaments. There was to be a 14-member Council of Ministers, including seven from each government, which would have executive and harmonising functions but would act by unanimity. It would have its own secretariat staffed by civil servants with a permanent headquarters, under a secretary general. Although its responsibilities were not initially defined, examples given were natural resources and the environment, agriculture, trade and industry, electricity generation, tourism, roads and transport, advisory health services, and sport, culture and the arts. Co-operation might later be extended to security.

The Belfast Agreement allowed for a possible joint parliamentary forum linking north and south. There was to be a North/South Ministerial Council, with a minimum of three members, two from Northern Ireland and one from the republic. There would be a secretariat and 'implementation bodies' to advance matters of common interest. Examples given for areas of co-operation included animal and plant health, teacher qualifications, transport planning, the environment, inland waterways, cross-border workers, tourism, EU programmes, inland fisheries, aquaculture, emergency services, and urban and rural development.

Notwithstanding the considerable difficulties in implementing other aspects of the agreement, progress on strand two was brisk and business-like, and contrasted sharply with the political difficulties that impeded the earlier experiments in the 20s and 70s. By the end of 1998, the broad shape of future arrangements was clear.

The December 1998 supplementary agreement

■ **B**ecause different components of the agreement interlock, progress on the specification of areas for north-south bodies and co-operation proceeded at the same pace as discussion of the establishment of the executive – and the issue of decommissioning of paramilitary weapons hindered progress on both. Nevertheless, outline agreement was finally reached on December 18th 1998 on the number and areas of responsibility of executive departments, and on the nature of north-south implementation bodies. The areas covered by the latter are listed in table 1.

In terms of the original list of 12 areas specified in the April 1998 agreement, three are missing from the list in table 1: social security/social welfare, inland fisheries, and urban and rural development. A further six were defined as areas for co-operation between existing bodies in Northern Ireland and the republic. The remaining three areas were targeted as ones in which implementation bodies were to be established. These were inland waterways, aquaculture and marine matters, and EU programmes. To these were added three other areas that had not been mentioned in the agreement: food safety, trade and business, and language.

This framework was not completed without resistance. There were reports of unionist opposition to the body on trade and business development, though not to that on language (which was regarded as mainly for nationalists). There was also a certain amount of bureaucratic resistance. Even before the agreement, co-operation in tourism promotion had given rise to difficulties, and there were reports that the Department of Agriculture and the Industrial Development Authority in the republic had reservations about the proposed form of co-operation. It is extremely unlikely that scepticism, or even outright hostility, in the republic to the strand-two bodies was confined to these departments or authorities.

Table 1: Inter-party agreement on areas for potential north-south co-operation and implementation

Area in Belfast Agreement	Outcome of December agreement
1. Agriculture – animal and plant health	Co-operation in agriculture
2. Education – teacher qualifications and exchanges	Co-operation in education
3. Transport – strategic transport planning	Co-operation in transport
4. Environment – environmental protection, pollution, water quality, and waste management	Co-operation in environment
5. Waterways – inland waterways	Implementation body for inland waterways
6. Social security/welfare – entitlements of cross-border workers and fraud control	No agreement
7. Tourism – promotion, marketing, research, and product development	Co-operation in tourism
8. Relevant EU Programmes such as SSPPR, INTERREG, Leader II and their successors	Implementation body for special EU programmes
9. Inland fisheries	No agreement
10. Aquaculture and marine matters	Implementation body for aquaculture and marine matters
11. Health – accident and emergency services and other related cross-border issues	Co-operation in health
12. Urban and rural development	No agreement
New area – agriculture: food safety	Implementation body for food safety
New area – economic development: trade and business	Implementation body for trade and business development
New area – language	Implementation body for language (Irish and Ulster Scots)

The implementation bodies

■ **T**he timetable for the establishment of the implementation bodies was closely linked to that of the other institutions provided for under the agreement, with the Stormont executive constituting the key. It was thus not until December 1999 that the first steps towards setting up the new bodies and the NSMC could be taken, but shortly afterwards they were temporarily consigned to limbo by the suspension of the devolved institutions.

The structure of the new bodies is described in table 2. At its apex lies the NSMC. It is intended that plenary sessions of the council, involving a number of members from the republic's government and from the Northern Ireland executive, would normally take place twice a year. It is envisaged that sectoral meetings (typically involving one minister from the republic, his or her counterpart from the northern executive and a political representative of the other northern 'tradition') will take place quarterly; these are to deal with specific areas within which co-operation or the establishment of an implementation body has been agreed. While the ministers attending these meetings have access to advice from civil servants within their departments, a crucial element is the secretariat servicing the new arrangements. Based in Armagh, this body was set up with a core of civil servants seconded from departments north and south.

Table 2: Projected staff and budgets of the north-south bodies

Implementation body	Staff	Budget (IR£)
Waterways Ireland	381	21.5
Food safety promotion board	25	6.5
Trade and business development	42	11.5
Special EU programmes	24	2.5*
Language	74	12.0
Foyle, Carlingford and Irish Lights	46	1.6
Total	592	55.6*

* not including 1 billion euros to be distributed in connection with EU programmes

The six bodies have certain features in common. Each is headed by a chief executive, typically under the direction of a board; its staff may be transferred or seconded from other bodies, or recruited directly; its budget is voted by the Dáil and the assembly; and it is required to produce an annual corporate plan, and an annual report. In addition to being answerable to the NSMC, it has a reporting relationship with the relevant ministers, with the Dail and with the assembly. Having said that, no two bodies have an identical formal structure. Most have a board appointed by the NSMC and drawn from the two jurisdictions, though some have none; and the relationship between the board and the chief executive varies.

The projected full staffing levels of the six bodies, together with their projected budgets for 2000, are indicated in table 2. Direct quantitative comparison between the bodies is difficult. They range in staff size from Waterways Ireland, which accounts for more than half the combined staff of all of the bodies, to the implementation body for special EU programmes, with the smallest projected staff (24). But the figures for budget size may be misleading. It is true that Waterways Ireland has the largest direct budget, but this is dwarfed by the budget for which the EU body is responsible: in addition to its allocation to cover its running costs, it is to implement programmes to the value of one billion euros.

Let us now turn to the individual bodies:

- **Waterways Ireland** is responsible for the 'management, maintenance, development and restoration of the inland navigable waterway system throughout the island', its obvious focus being recreational. It assumed many of the functions of, inter alia, the Waterways Service of the republic's Department of Arts, Heritage, Gaeltacht and the Islands and the Rivers Agency of the Department of Agriculture in the north.

- The **food safety** body is responsible for promotion of food safety, research, communication of food alerts, surveillance of food-borne diseases, promotion of scientific co-operation and linkages between laboratories, and development of cost-effective facilities for specialised laboratory testing. Its terrain is not uncontested: it is required to work in association with the food safety agencies of the UK and the republic, which retain important inspection rights.

- The **trade and business development** body is to 'exchange information and co-ordinate work on trade, business development and related matters, in areas where the two administrations specifically agree it would be in their mutual interest'. Its underlying purpose is to promote economic development, especially by encouraging north-south trade.

- The **special EU programmes** body was given a wide range of responsibilities, including co-ordination of existing programmes, advising the governments on further applications, preparation of detailed applications, and assistance in the administration of existing programmes at a range of levels.

- The **language** body was given responsibility for two areas: first, for a range of activities already carried out in the republic (including promotion of Irish in a variety of ways) now extended to the north; and, secondly, for the 'promotion of greater awareness and use of Ullans and of Ulster Scots cultural issues, both within Northern Ireland and throughout the island'.

- The **Foyle, Carlingford and Irish Lights** body replaced a number of agencies, and was given responsibility for the promotion of Lough Foyle and Carlingford Lough in commerce, recreation and fisheries; it was also given responsibility for aquaculture, marine tourism and lighthouses.

The north-south bodies in context

■ The mechanics of the new bodies tell us little about their political significance. To what extent do they correspond with the hopes of nationalists and the fears of unionists? When set against the size of the central civil service in the republic and the north, or even when compared with local government, the staffs of the north-south bodies are tiny. When compared with national or local-government budgets, their allocation is insignificant. When compared with the domains of activity of central and local authorities, their responsibilities are marginal. It would thus be premature to describe them as the core of a new level of government (as this is understood in multi-level structures such as federal ones) in any meaningful sense. But the implementation bodies are not the full story. The agreement also provided for areas of north-south 'co-operation', and here progress has been much slower. It is true that in agriculture, education and tourism programmes of co-operation have been agreed – with a concrete outcome in the last in the shape of a planned all-Ireland tourism agency. But there are other areas where political considerations have impeded progress. Transport is the most obvious: notwithstanding the normal priority of geographical arguments over political ones in transport planning, the intended co-operation has not taken place. The relevant ministry in the north is in the hands of the Democratic Unionist Party, which has so far refused to cooperate – an illustration of the failure of the agreement to proof itself against particular forms of political resistance.

The model implicit in the new north-south arrangements is the strategy of functional co-operation so intimately associated with European integration, based on the assumption that political accommodation will be facilitated by establishing intense patterns of contact between élites. The EU is, indeed, a remarkable testimony of the capacity of determined élites to push through radical political change in the face of indifference or even hostility.

By comparison with attitudes towards Europe, hostility to Irish unity may be more intense, if confined to one clearly defined section of the island. Sympathy for unity is probably uneven, and indifference is the norm, especially in the republic. But the crucial question is the perspective of the relevant élites. While there are politicians and public servants in the republic and in Northern Ireland driven by the goal of Irish unity, the reality is that for most of the former Brussels takes priority over Belfast, while for most of the latter London takes precedence over Dublin.

11

The British-Irish Council

Elizabeth Meehan

History of the idea

■ The idea of modern confederal institutions in Great Britain and Ireland (as a whole or north and south) has been around since Gladstone. On the agendas of the Scottish National Party and Plaid Cymru for some decades, with little hope of success, recent events have given it practical expression – in a new form.[1] This arises from devolution in the United Kingdom and the multi-party Belfast Agreement, with its concomitant British-Irish Treaty of December 2nd 1999.

The British-Irish Council, outlined in 'strand three' of the agreement, links the Republic of Ireland, the UK, devolved institutions in Wales, Northern Ireland and Scotland, and the crown dependencies (or territories) of the Channel Islands and the Isle of Man[2] into what the taoiseach, Bertie Ahern, described in an Edinburgh lecture in October 1998 as 'a loose confederation'.

Different, in the context of an independent Ireland and asymmetrical
UK devolution, from the 'home rule all round' mooted by some in
the early part of the last century, the BIC can be seen, in the words of
the UUP assembly member Esmond Birnie at an Encounter
conference on the body in December 1998 (Encounter, nd), as an
expression of the 'human truth' of the mosaic of relationships
amongst the peoples of the islands.

'Post-nationalists', 'new unionists' or neither who share this sense
of the BIC prefer a different name for it, most often the 'council of
the isles' (Hassan and Wilson, 1999: 7), to reflect the complexities of
overlapping identifications, mutual interests, interdependence and
shared sovereignty. The name British-Irish Council may imply the
prioritising of identities and interests that are binary opposites and
mutually exclusive. This construction is consistent with seeing the
BIC as a mere placatory response to a late proposal at the talks from
the UUP for an institution to counter-balance the seeming
reunification dynamic of the North/South Ministerial Council – and
of little interest to the government of the Republic of Ireland.[3] That
key participants, from different political backgrounds, do not, or no
longer, see the BIC simply as a 'bargaining chip' bodes well for its
future. But its promise depends on how the provisions of the
agreement are fleshed out and unresolved issues handled.

The agreement

■ **'S**trand three' of the agreement established the BIC 'to promote
the harmonious and mutually beneficial development of the totality
of relationships among the peoples of these islands'.

As noted, it comprises representatives of the London and Dublin
governments, devolved institutions, the crown dependencies and,
potentially, elected regional assemblies in England. The agreement
specifies summit meetings twice a year and regular sectoral or cross-

sectoral meetings among relevant ministers, accountable according to the rules of their own institutions.

Its role is to 'exchange information, discuss, consult and use best endeavours to reach agreement on matters of mutual interest within the competence of the relevant administrations'. Suggested topics include: transport links, agriculture, the environment, culture, health, education and approaches to EU matters. The BIC may agree, normally consensually, upon common policies or actions, from which individual members, however, may opt out. Financial support for its actions is to be agreed and provided by its members. The governments in London and Dublin, in co-ordination with officials of the other members, provide the secretariat.

The agreement also permits two or more members to develop bilateral or multilateral arrangements to enable consultation, co-operation and joint decision-making, subject to competence. Such arrangements will not require the prior approval of the BIC and will operate independently.

Outside BIC structures but related to them, the agreement proposes a network of parliamentary links, upon which the British-Irish Interparliamentary Body has started work. It also replaces the 1985 Anglo-Irish Agreement's institutions with a new British-Irish Intergovernmental Conference, for co-operation over bilateral common interests and mutual concerns with respect to non-devolved matters in Northern Ireland.

Fleshing out the agreement

■ In February 1999, the then Northern Ireland political development minister, Paul Murphy, made proposals to the region's parties for a BIC agenda. They were considered during that year, for most of which the assembly was still in 'shadow' mode. In the brief first period of devolution, the inaugural BIC summit was held in

London in December 1999. Because of the suspension in February 2000, and diary problems, no further plenary meeting had occurred at the time of writing.

At the first meeting, however, a programme of work and associated responsibilities were agreed. Tackling drugs was prioritised and the lead given to the republic's government. Social exclusion and the development of an anti-poverty strategy for Britain and Ireland were taken on by Wales and Scotland. Northern Ireland is overseeing the development of a transport strategy for the islands; the Isle of Man and the Channel Islands are taking the lead on the 'knowledge economy'; and the UK government leads on the environment. The handling of emissions from Sellafield, about which there is a conflict of interest between the UK government and all other BIC partners (except, perhaps, the Channel Islands), remains to be attested to.

Though all these topics have EU aspects, tackling EU matters is not explicitly part of the current programme. Nor are other concrete and salient issues, suggested by parties and other observers in 1998 and 1999 – such as agriculture, culture and sport, education, tourism, countering sectarianism and racism, the establishment or reinforcement of city and community networks for joint research and lesson-learning, the name of the institution, the nature of its secretariat and civic participation.

Unresolved issues

■ To some people, the most apocalyptic unresolved issue is whether the BIC – paradoxically, given its unionist connotations at birth – is more likely than the NSMC to encourage the break-up of the UK.[4] The crown dependencies, initially surprised by not being consulted about their inclusion, decided that being included was an acknow-ledgement of their independence. Interest, particularly in Scotland, in autonomous relations with the republic – and the EU – is palpable, as seen in the enthusiasm in Scottish political circles for the establishment by the republic of a consulate general in Edinburgh (as in Cardiff) in 1998, fostering business, academic and cultural exchanges, and assisting presidential and ministerial visits.

Scottish enjoyment of direct links with the republic can embarrass the Dublin government[5] – keen to maintain an unprecedentedly close relationship, now transcending Northern Ireland, with London. The health of the relationship – at least until the rift when the UK government suspended the assembly and part of a British document unflatteringly describing the then new Dublin foreign minister was leaked – is evidenced in the speech by the prime minister, Tony Blair, to the Oireachtas, and reactions to it, in November 1998. The taoiseach, during his visit to Edinburgh in October 1998, steered a careful course between the Scylla of denying that what had been good for the republic could be good also for Scotland and the Charybdis of endorsing a claim for independence.

Nevertheless, the taoiseach told the people of Scotland, on St Andrew's Day 1999, that he welcomed not only the BIC but also its 'ample scope' for bilateral relations, and he was 'keen to exploit the potential of the new political dimension' (Irish Times, Scotsman, November 30th 1999). Potential exploitation of the BIC by Scotland to assert quasi-independence is a concern to the UK government. Its Memorandum of Understanding on the BIC's operation states firmly that all relations with foreign governments must be channelled through the Foreign Office (Financial Times, October 15th 1999) and this is confirmed in the 1999 concordat on dealings with the EU.

But the language of pluralism and interdependence in the articles and speeches of key participants, such as those mentioned, and the (recently resigned) Scottish National Party leader, Alex Salmond, suggests that the apocalyptic vision is not on the agenda for the foreseeable future. The BIC's potential impact more likely lies in the cross-fertilisation of policy ideas and practice and a renaissance of cultural commonalities. Both of these, of course, already happen in all directions – for the reasons of human geography and history noted by Mr Birnie.

Civic links, like those fostered by the republic's consul general in Edinburgh (Irish Times, Scotsman, November 30th 1999), make 'the totality of relationships among the peoples of the islands' more like the 'bottom-up' underpinnings of the Nordic Council with which the BIC is often compared (Hassan and Wilson, 1999: 10-11). But if the BIC is, indeed, to be the badge of Mr Birnie's 'human truth' and not an emptied symbol, several problems, ignored in or unanticipated by the agreement, need to be addressed.

First, there is the glaring absence of representatives of English authorities and the disconcerting assumption by the British government that English interests and aspirations could be reflected adequately by a minister for regions in an executive with a UK-wide remit. Even if something else can be done – perhaps observer status for the English regional development agencies (forerunners, perhaps, of elected assemblies) – other problems remain.

The character of the BIC may be swamped by a plethora of other innovations. In addition to the Memorandum of Understanding and interdepartmental concordats, these comprise:

- the Joint Ministerial Committee, established in July 1998 to co-ordinate the UK and devolved governments;
- the allocation of a constitutional arbitrator role to the Judicial Committee of the Privy Council; and
- partial reform of the Lords, with the potential to become, in part, a chamber of territorial representation.

The question arises as to whether the existence of all these regulators of internal relationships means that the BIC, including the 'foreign' partner,[6] may be restricted in its deliberations to issues with a clearly Irish dimension.

Whether a strict constitutional construction emerges, there are other reasons for suspecting that the BIC's agenda could be more exclusively state-driven than in the Nordic Council and, more particularly – given the Dublin government's sensitivity to constitutional delicacies in Britain – UK state-driven. (And if driven by both states, what then of the relationship with the British-Irish Intergovernmental Conference?) The first post-agreement indications of the BIC's programme came from the British Cabinet Office in 1998 and a UK minister in 1999, Northern Irish 'shadow' ministers being invited to react to them.

Northern Ireland unionists are concerned about discrepancies between the NSMC and BIC budgets and secretariats. Their concerns are equally relevant to all who want the BIC to live up to its potential for 'the peoples of these islands'. A small, under-funded secretariat located in the largest BIC partner's capital is inauspicious for the growth of an institution able to control its own agenda, based on its knowledge of what people want, and which meets aspirations effectively. The smaller BIC partners have suggested that the secretariat be located in the same place as the rotating presidency or occupy a permanent site outside London – in Glasgow, perhaps, because of its place at the hub of many cross-cutting north, south, east and west connections. Neither idea has found favour yet.

Finally, the agreement does not institutionalise civic participation in constructing the BIC's agenda, as it does with the assembly's Civic Forum and the mooted possibility of a similar north-south body. There is no shortage, on either side of the Irish Sea, of non-governmental organisations well-placed to advise the BIC about how best to link the executive(s) and the people(s).

Bibliography

Encounter (nd), Strand III – The British Irish Council, report of a round-table discussion at Wilton Park, Sussex, December 4th-6th 1998

Hassan, G and Wilson, R (1999), The British-Irish Council as a Multi-Form Organisation, Edinburgh: Centre for Scottish Public Policy

Notes to the text

[1] The best-known non-partisan proponents of the idea are Richard Kearney and Simon Partridge. They and partisan proponents are discussed in Hassan and Wilson (1999).

[2] The agreement also opens the possibility of representatives of elected English regional assemblies, if they are established. Whether this applies to the newly elected mayor of London is not yet clear.

[3] On early lack of interest (and changes) on the part of the republic, see comments by Walter Kirwan, Department of the Taoiseach in Encounter (nd: 11).

[4] Such a prediction was made by an anti-agreement unionist at a conference in Scotland in January 1999 on Scotland in the British union and in the EU.

[5] Again note the comments by Walter Kirwan reported in Encounter (nd: 11).

[6] Under British law, the republic is not a foreign country. Recognised as independent, not now in the Commonwealth, it occupies its own category, distinct from the general class of non-Commonwealth countries; its nationals, while not British, are also not aliens.

12

Human rights and equality
Colin Harvey

Introduction

■ **H**uman rights and equality are central to the new structures of governance in Northern Ireland. Given the historical context, this is unsurprising. The agreement contains impressive references to the legal protection of these values. Its Declaration of Support includes a commitment to the 'protection and vindication of the human rights of all' as well as to 'partnership, equality and mutual respect'.

The agreement, however, is not entirely consistent on rights matters. For example, the reference to vindication of the human rights of all in the declaration may be contrasted with the rather narrow language – respect for the identity and ethos of both communities – adopted in relation to the bill of rights. The tensions expressed in these inconsistencies will work themselves out in the years ahead.

People in Northern Ireland, as elsewhere, disagree about almost every aspect of social, political and cultural life. The challenge for the new democratic structures is to respect disagreement and ensure decisions are not removed from full public discussion. For the value which underpins the agreement is self-government and the primary right is the right to participate.

Thus, respect for the principles of the agreement requires rather less faith in the courts than is usual. There is no necessary connection between the protection of human rights and equality and judicial enforcement. It is the easy option, of course, but not the one that accords best with modern conceptions of democratic citizenship.

Constitutional context

■ **T**he agreement must be viewed in the context of broader constitutional changes in the UK, the Republic of Ireland and beyond. This is not to argue that it can be reduced to 'external' factors; it had its own dynamics within Northern Ireland. For example, in relation to human rights there was a prior consensus on the need for some form of protection. On equality, civil society had been very active on the issue. There was momentum for change in these areas. The problem was the absence of a constitutional settlement and the belief that legal protection could only follow from this.

But, looking to the wider constitutional context, the election of a Labour government in May 1997, with a substantial majority, was significant for two reasons. First, the government was more pragmatic in its approach to Northern Ireland. Secondly, it was a government comfortable with the language of human rights and equality, as evidenced by the Human Rights Act 1998 giving further effect to the European Convention on Human Rights in domestic law. The act, which entered into force on October 2nd 2000, enables individuals to enforce their convention rights before domestic courts. It also structures the legislative competence of the Northern Ireland

Assembly. With this openness to human-rights discourse, it was easier to ensure human rights played a significant part in devolution to Northern Ireland.

Devolution more broadly is another aspect of Labour government policy which made an impact on Northern Ireland. For example, it became almost impossible to argue sensibly for full integration of the region into the UK – as had some unionists – when decentralisation was becoming the norm. In the republic, the willingness to envisage constitutional change in relation to articles 2 and 3 was also important: constitutional change was on the agenda in both states. Beyond these islands, it is arguable European developments played their part in encouraging post-national thinking – in particular, by opening up space for constitutional experimentation involving interlocking relationships. All this, to some extent, shaped the human rights and equality agenda which emerged.

Human rights, equality and the assembly

UK constitutional arrangements effectively permit Westminster to bind the devolved administrations. Parliament remains the supreme legislature and the devolved administrations are treated rather like unruly children, with firm ground-rules laid down. Constitutional conventions may quickly emerge to temper this relationship, but in strict constitutional law Westminster retains its power to legislate for the UK as a whole.

The legislative competence of the assembly is limited by the European Convention on Human Rights, European Community law and the prohibition of religious and political discrimination.[1] If a provision of an act of the assembly violates the relevant aspects of the convention, it is outside its legislative competence; all bills proposed by the assembly thus need to be proofed against convention rights. This should ensure that rights considerations are addressed early. Ministers and Northern

Ireland departments are also limited in relation to making, confirming or approving subordinate legislation or doing any act which conflicts with EC law or the convention.[2] Discrimination on ground of religious belief or political opinion is also prohibited.[3]

There are entrenched enactments which further constrain the assembly, its ministers and departments. For example, no modification of the Human Rights Act 1998 is permitted.[4] The approach is thus to structure the competence of the devolved institutions by human rights and anti-discrimination provisions. As the European Union develops its own human rights and equality protections, these curbs on legislative competence will become more important. In addition, all ministers are required to affirm the 'pledge of office',[5] which inter alia commits them 'to serve all the people of Northern Ireland equally, and to act in accordance with the general obligations on government to promote equality and prevent discrimination'.[6]

It will be important to ensure that human rights and equality norms are brought into the mainstream of the legislative process and public administration. On this the human-rights directorate of the Office of the First and Deputy First Minister (OFMDFM) has an important role in raising awareness of human rights within the administration. The assembly's 'Committee of the Centre' will also have a vital role in scrutinising effectively the work of the OFMDFM.

All these efforts will be improved if the assembly adopts a creative approach in using the resources and experience of other statutory bodies and the community and voluntary sector. An inclusive approach to tapping that knowledge can ensure the assembly's work is compatible with democratic values.

Enforcing human rights and equality

■ **O**ne way to promote human rights and equality is through dedicated statutory bodies. There is both a Northern Ireland Human

Rights Commission and an Equality Commission for Northern Ireland. These are not entirely new creations: on human rights they were preceded by the Standing Advisory Commission on Human Rights and on equality by, among others, the Fair Employment Commission for Northern Ireland and the Equal Opportunities Commission for Northern Ireland. It is the scope of the functions and powers of the new bodies that is different.

From a human-rights perspective one of the most significant elements of the new order is the Human Rights Commission. It has attracted considerable attention and one wonders whether its work will encourage other such commissions in the UK. As part of the agreement, an Irish Human Rights Commission is also being established and the republic's government has committed itself to equivalent human-rights protection.

The Northern Ireland commission has a chief commissioner, Prof Brice Dickson, and nine part-time commissioners. It is charged with keeping under review the adequacy and effectiveness in the region of law and practice relating to human rights.[7] It has an advisory role vis-à-vis the secretary of state and the Executive Committee on legislative and other measures to protect human rights.[8] It must also promote awareness and understanding of human rights.[9] While it possesses the power to launch investigations, this is limited by the absence of any power to compel witnesses or discover documents.[10] Individuals may apply to the commission for assistance[11] and it can bring proceedings involving law or practice relating to protection of human rights.[12]

One of the more important functions of the commission is the bill of rights exercise. It is tasked with consulting and advising on the scope for defining in Westminster legislation a bill of rights for Northern Ireland. The rights must be supplementary to the convention and reflect the particular circumstances of Northern Ireland. The instrument must draw as appropriate on international instruments and experience. The rights are to 'reflect the principles of mutual respect for the identity and ethos of both communities and parity of esteem'. Much is at stake here: detailed thought will have to be given to which rights should be 'constitutionalised' and to gearing the process to the overall objectives of the agreement.

The commission can play an important role in the protection of human rights in Northern Ireland. It is a useful resource for the assembly and close co-operation should help ensure that potential violations of human rights are spotted at an early stage.

The debate on equality has had a life of its own and is not solely a product of the political process. While there was much opposition to the creation of a unified Equality Commission, this is nevertheless the result.[13] The commission replaces the Fair Employment Commission for Northern Ireland, the Equal Opportunities Commission for Northern Ireland, the Commission for Racial Equality for Northern Ireland and the Northern Ireland Disability Council.[14] Although there is institutional unity, the body of equality and anti-discrimination law however remains distinct. The commission has a chief commissioner, Joan Harbison, a deputy chief commissioner, Bronagh Hinds, and 18 part-time commissioners.

The measure which has attracted most attention is the section 75 equality duty contained in the Northern Ireland Act 1998. This places a statutory duty on public authorities, when carrying out their functions, to have due regard to the need to promote equality of opportunity between: persons of different religious belief, political opinion, racial group, age, marital status or sexual orientation; men and women generally; persons with a disability and persons without; and persons with dependants and persons without.[15] In carrying out its functions the public authority must also have regard to good relations between persons of different religious belief, political opinion or racial group.[16]

The innovation comes in the provisions on enforcement. The Equality Commission has the function of keeping under review the duties imposed under section 75, as well as offering advice to public authorities.[17] Central to this is the equality scheme which a designated public authority is required to submit to the commission. The scheme must include arrangements for:

- assessing compliance with the duty and consultation;
- assessing and consulting on the likely impact of policies adopted on promotion of equality of opportunity;
- monitoring the adverse impact of policies adopted on equality of opportunity;
- publishing assessments;
- training staff; and
- ensuring access to information and services provided by the authority.[18]

Before the submission of a scheme the authority is required to consult with, for example, affected groups.[19] The commission has the power to approve the scheme or refer it to the secretary of state.[20]

This is one of the most interesting aspects of post-agreement life in Northern Ireland. It goes a step further than human-rights law by attempting to build learning processes into public administration. The inclusion of affected groups brings wider participation in the process of decision-making, transferring the experience of these groups into public administration. The obligation on designated public bodies to conduct impact assessments is another aspect of this. It is an example how, in law at least, precise mechanisms can be devised to try to make equality a mainstream feature of public administration. Valuable lessons will be gained from this experience in Northern Ireland.

Conclusion

■ **T**he agreement has given official recognition to the importance of the promotion of human rights and equality in Northern Ireland. The legal order that has followed contains some highly innovative provisions. The experience will no doubt be watched anxiously by those across the UK, Ireland and beyond. There is little room for complacency. This will be particularly true in the human-rights sphere. While everyone now 'talks the talk', clarity is often lacking.

Reasonable people disagree fundamentally about the meaning of human rights and this raises the issue of who decides. The assumption is often that these matters should be resolved by the courts. But must this be so? Would it not be odd indeed, having just secured a settlement based on the fundamental right to participate, to remove issues indefinitely from resolution through dialogue in the public political sphere? Courts, of course, have their place but care must be taken to ensure that the struggle for democratic inclusion in Northern Ireland does not result in the removal of many issues from public deliberation and resolution. We should be much more aware of all the other mechanisms to promote human rights and equality if we really want to take these values seriously (Waldron, 1999).

Bibliography

Waldron, J (1999), Law and Disagreement, Oxford: Clarendon Press

Notes to the text

[1] Northern Ireland Act 1998 s. 6(2)

[2] Northern Ireland Act 1999 s. 24

[3] Northern Ireland Act 1999 s. 24. In addition, they are also prohibited from aiding or inciting another person to discriminate on the ground of religious belief or political opinion.

[4] Northern Ireland Act 1998 s. 7(1)(b)

[5] Northern Ireland Act 1998 s. 16(4)(b), 17(8), schedule 4

[6] Northern Ireland Act 1998 schedule 4

[7] Northern Ireland Act 1998 s. 6(1)

[8] Northern Ireland Act 1998 s. 69(3)

[9] Northern Ireland Act 1998 s. 69(6)

[10] Northern Ireland Act 1998 s. 69(8)

[11] Northern Ireland Act 1998 s. 69(5)(a) and s. 70

[12] Northern Ireland Act 1998 s. 69(5)(b)

[13] Northern Ireland Act 1998 s. 73

[14] Northern Ireland Act 1998 s. 74

[15] Northern Ireland Act 1998 s. 75(1)

[16] Northern Ireland Act 1998 s. 75(2)

[17] Northern Ireland Act 1998 schedule 9 para. 1(a) and (b)

[18] Northern Ireland Act 1998 schedule 9 para. 4

[19] Northern Ireland Act 1998 schedule 9 para. 5

[20] Northern Ireland 1998 schedule 9 para. 6

Security, justice and independent commissions

Dominic Bryan

Introduction

■ **U**nder the Belfast Agreement Northern Ireland remains a part of the United Kingdom until a majority of its people, through a referendum, deems otherwise. As such, certain responsibilities, particularly in relation to international obligations and defence, remain with the Westminster parliament. However certain issues, specifically those relating to the security of the UK – including policing, criminal justice and the decommissioning of paramilitary weapons – received particular attention in the agreement.

Issues of national security within Northern Ireland are still the responsibility of the Northern Ireland Office and the secretary of state, who lays legislation before Westminster and maintains a place in the cabinet. These are among the 'reserved' or non-devolved matters. The Northern Ireland secretary may give approval to the assembly to legislate in reserved areas in the future; certain policing powers will, in effect, reside with political representatives in the region. In addition, under the agreement, 'in recognition of the Irish Government's special interest in Northern Ireland', a regular British-Irish Intergovernmental Conference is to meet, at which Dublin can put forward views and proposals on non-devolved matters.

These issues are important, as they are likely to remain central political problems. They provide a focus for different perceptions of the Belfast Agreement. They raise fundamental questions about the legitimacy of Northern Ireland as part of the UK and the 'war' fought by the IRA; in particular, they raise the issue of the legitimate use of physical force.

Unionists, keen to see the agreement as a settlement with Northern Ireland's placed in the UK secure, want to protect the legitimacy of existing policing and justice arrangements, demand the decommissioning of paramilitary weapons and remain sceptical about the merits of the accelerated release of paramilitary prisoners. Nationalists, and particularly republicans, view the agreement as leading to intensified political links with the Republic of Ireland. For them reform of policing and justice and the release of prisoners represent an acceptance of the essentially political nature of the conflict.

To deal with these issues a number of independent commissions, reviews and enquiries were set up.

Policing

■ In recognition of the difficulty of securing agreement on policing, the Belfast Agreement set the terms of reference for an independent commission that was chaired by the former Conservative Party chair, cabinet minister and governor of Hong Kong, Chris Patten. It was to look into future arrangements for policing in Northern Ireland, 'including means of encouraging widespread support for those arrangements' . A New Beginning: Policing in Northern Ireland – The Report of the Independent Commission on Policing for Northern Ireland ('the Patten report') was published in September 1999 and made 175 recommendations. The key elements were:

- developing a human-rights-based approach to policing in Northern Ireland;
- making 'policing with the community' a 'core function' of the police service;
- developing accountability through both a 19-member Police Board (including 10 assembly members from parties comprising the Executive Committee) and District Policing Partnership Boards established by each district council;
- the appointment of a powerful police ombudsman to deal with complaints;
- a system of recruitment designed quickly to boost the number of Catholics in the police service, while the service would be reduced from around 13,000 officers to around 7,500;
- the maintenance of a neutral working environment and the adoption of a new name (Northern Ireland Police Service) and a new badge; and
- an oversight commissioner to report publicly on progress achieved.

The report clearly fell short of demands by SF to disband the RUC and the republicans waited to see how the British government would implement the proposals. The SDLP welcomed Patten but had growing reservations after the publication by the NIO of an implementation plan in June 2000. The UUP reacted particularly to the renaming of the RUC and a campaign to save the name soon developed among unionists and some former members of the force. In short, as expected, policing remained a key, unresolved political issue even after the passge of the Police (Northern Ireland) Act in November 2000.

While policing is to remain under the remit of the Northern Ireland secretary, it is clearly possible – indeed envisaged – that day-to-day running of the police service should be moved closer to communities and be accountable within the region. This will, in all likelihood, depend on to what extent the SDLP and SF become involved in the new Police Board and the District Policing Partnership Boards.

Justice and victims

■ **P**articipants in the Belfast Agreement agreed that the criminal-justice system should:

- deliver a fair and impartial system of justice to the community;
- be responsive to communities' concerns, and encourage community involvement where appropriate;
- have the confidence of all parts of the community; and
- deliver justice efficiently and effectively.

A review of the criminal-justice system, other than areas involving emergency legislation, was set up under the agreement. It reported in March 2000 (Criminal Justice Review Group, 2000) but received far less political attention than the Patten report. The review similarly made international standards of human rights central to its work. Its recommendations were wide-ranging and included:

- a strategy to ensure that the workforce in the criminal-justice system reflects the community in Northern Ireland:
- strategies to increase confidence in the Department of the Director of Public Prosecutions;
- procedures for ensuring judicial independence;

- a Law Commission for Northern Ireland to keep civil and criminal law under review;
- a Northern Ireland-based Judicial Appointments Commission appointed by the first and deputy first ministers;
- an increased role for lay people in adjudication;
- a system of restorative justice as part of the formal justice process and subject to the full range of human-rights protections;
- a community-safety strategy, including a central-government Community Safety Unit and Community Safety and Policing Partnerships;
- a higher priority for victims within the criminal-justice system; and
- exploration of co-operation between criminal-justice agencies north and south.

The tenor of the proposals was that the justice system should work at a community and a regional level. The review foresaw several justice matters being devolved to the assembly and a Department of Justice being established. In addition, the introduction of the Human Rights Act in October 2000 and the likely introduction of a bill of rights for Northern Ireland, after a process of consultation by the Human Rights Commission, will mean that a wider range of issues are likely to be decided by the courts in the region. One obvious example would be disputes over parades, currently dealt with by the Parades Commission.

Yet issues of justice are far more wide-ranging than simply the justice system. A central problem for the assembly will be dealing with the past. The Northern Ireland Victims Commission, established before the agreement, reported shortly after it, and implementation of policy on victims now falls to the Office of the First and Deputy First Minister and its Victims Liaison Unit. A wide spectrum of pressure groups are attempting to get past injustices investigated, so that the 'troubles' will be continually revisited on the political stage. The 'Bloody Sunday' tribunal might be the most high-profile attempt to deal with the past, so far, but it is not likely to be the last.

Decommissioning and security

■ **D**ecommissioning of paramilitary weapons has been the most divisive issue since the agreement. It was responsible for the delay in the setting up of the Executive Committee, and for the suspension of the assembly from February to May 2000; and it remains the most likely issue on which the executive might collapse. It strikes at the heart of the status of Northern Ireland – symbolising as it does, from different perspectives, the legitimacy of the 'armed struggle' or the British presence in Ireland.

Under the agreement all participants 'reaffirm their commitment to the total disarmament of all paramilitary weapons', with an Independent International Commission on Decommissioning set up under the Canadian general John de Chastelain. Unionists consistently argued subsequently that the IRA had not done enough, while SF pointed out that under the agreement all it as a political party was required to do was to 'use any influence they may have' to achieve decommissioning. On May 6th 2000 the IRA announced it would allow independent verification of the security of some of its arms dumps.

Politically linked to decommissioning, although not directly linked in the agreement, was the undertaking by the British government in the latter to 'make progress towards the objective of as early a return as possible to normal security arrangements in Northern Ireland, consistent with the level of threat'. Among the objectives were the removal of security installations, reviewing regulations on legally held firearms and, more critically, the possible removal of emergency powers.

Balancing rights and freedoms

■ **E**mergency powers have governed policing and security in Northern Ireland since the introduction of the Civil Authorities (Special Powers) Act in 1922. The bomb at Omagh on August 15th 1998, planted by the 'Real IRA' and killing 29 people, led the London and Dublin governments to introduce yet more legislation. It is likely that dissident republican and loyalist groups will engage in violence in the future and there will be significant political pressure on London and Dublin to maintain specific security measures.

There are, however, clear inconsistencies between such security measures and the introduction of the Human Rights Act and a future Northern Ireland bill of rights, as well as the British government's commitment to return to 'normal' security arrangements. Creating a justice system where rights and freedoms are protected, while dealing with pressures deriving from the threat from paramilitary groups, will be a central task for administrations in London, Belfast and Dublin over the years to come.

Bibliography

Criminal Justice Review Group (2000), Review of the Criminal Justice System in Northern Ireland, Belfast: Stationery Office

14
Devolved and retained powers

Tom Hadden

■ **T**he Belfast Agreement, as implemented by the Northern Ireland Act 1998, is the fourth exercise in the devolution of legislative and executive powers to Northern Ireland. The first was the Government of Ireland Act 1920, under which the Ulster Unionist Party dominated the Northern Ireland Parliament and government from 1921 to 1972. The second was the brief period of power-sharing in 1974 under the terms of the Northern Ireland Act 1973. The third was the abortive attempt at 'rolling devolution' under the Northern Ireland Act 1982. This latest exercise has been influenced not only by these previous attempts but also by the parallel devolution structures for Scotland and Wales.

Transferred, reserved and excepted powers

■ **T**he 1998 act provides for three distinct categories of powers: transferred, reserved and excepted. Put simply, transferred powers are those that have already been devolved to the Northern Ireland Assembly and executive; reserved powers are those that are not currently devolved but could be in the future if the new institutions prove stable and effective; and excepted powers are those regarded as necessarily the preserve of the central government and parliament in London. Excepted and reserved powers are set out in detail in schedules 2 and 3 of the act and transferred powers are then defined as anything not excepted or reserved (section 4).

In practical terms, transferred powers cover all those matters which since 1973 were dealt with by the old Northern Ireland departments: agriculture, health and social services, education, the environment, planning and local government, employment and economic development, and finance and personnel in respect of those functions. These have been reallocated from the six departments of direct rule into ten new departments, each with its own minister and supervising assembly committee.

Reserved powers include all those devolved between 1921 and 1972 but subsequently the responsibility of the Northern Ireland Office – notably criminal law, the police, public order, emergency powers and the courts. The international commissions to review policing and criminal justice, established under the Belfast Agreement, both concluded that in due course these functions should be devolved.

The list of reserved powers, however, also includes matters that were not previously devolved – such as banking and financial services, postal services, telecommunications, and certain import and export controls. It is not clear whether there is any immediate intention of devolving these powers, which would clearly give a greater degree of independence to the assembly and executive, not least in their relations with the republic.

Excepted powers cover all those matters regarded as the prerogative of a sovereign state – such as international relations, national defence, national security, nationality, Parliament, elections and taxation.

There are, however, certain exemptions, notably in respect of international relations to facilitate the assembly and executive in their dealings with the republic.

Additional limitations

■ **T**here are a number of additional constraints on the assembly and the executive which cover all devolved powers and are paralleled in the devolution legislation for Scotland and Wales. There are express provisions invalidating any legislation or administrative action that contravenes the European Convention on Human Rights or the law of the European Union or that discriminates on the ground of religious belief or political opinion (sections 6 and 76). There is also a reserve power for the UK government to prohibit or direct any executive action by a Northern Ireland minister, in so far as that is required in order to comply with the UK's international obligations (section 26). This is supplemented by an express power to impose quotas in respect of Northern Ireland's contribution to the performance of international undertakings by the UK government (section 27).

If any dispute arises in respect of the formal competence of the assembly or executive, there is express provision for the matter to be referred to the Northern Ireland Court of Appeal and ultimately to the Judicial Committee of the Privy Council (section 79). These provisions are parallel to those on 'devolution issues' in the comparable legislation for Scotland and Wales.

Financial control

■ **I**t follows from the inclusion of all forms of taxation in the category of excepted powers that the assembly and executive are in practice wholly dependent on the UK government in respect of overall public expenditure. There is no formal legislative provision on allocation of resources by the Treasury between reserved and devolved functions and it is therefore open to Westminster, acting through the Northern Ireland secretary, to make what allocation it pleases to Northern Ireland out of central funds (section 58). The situation in respect of Scotland and Wales is the same.

The powers of the devolved assemblies and executives are therefore limited to the allocation of whatever block grant is made to them. These grants have for many years been calculated on the basis of the 'Barnett formula' (see chapter 18). But the Treasury may at any time alter the formula or make specific allocations in respect of particular circumstances. There will therefore remain considerable scope for bargaining between central government and all three devolved administrations as to the size – and, in practice, the use – of these annual block grants.

Distinctive structures

■ **D**espite these various parallels in devolution to Northern Ireland, Scotland and Wales, there are significant differences. The most obvious is that the Welsh National Assembly has no powers of primary legislation, though it has control over secondary orders and instruments issued by the Welsh Executive. There are also some differences in the legislative powers devolved to Scotland and Northern Ireland. There is no equivalent in Scotland to the powers that have been 'reserved' vis-à-vis Northern Ireland (though the Scottish legislation uses the term 'reserved matters' to refer to what are called 'excepted matters' in the Northern Ireland Act). And there is specific provision for the Northern Ireland Assembly to legislate on reserved matters with the consent of the secretary of state.

The peculiar constitutional and political status of the constituent parts of the UK has thus been preserved. So has the overriding

constitutional authority of the Westminster parliament, subject only
to some arguable limitations in the Scottish and Irish Acts of Union.
No attempt has been made to impose uniformity or introduce formal
federal structures common in other composite jurisdictions.

an agreeable future?

15

The people's verdict

Sydney Elliott

The referendum

■ **T**he third element of the 'triple lock' promised by the government required that the Belfast Agreement, made by politicians and parties, be endorsed by the public. It was hailed as the first simultaneous all-Ireland ballot since 1918 (an assertion which ignored successive European elections since 1979).

Officially this was an issue to be decided by the electorate of Northern Ireland but, given the investment by government in the talks, it was not uninterested. The Northern Ireland Office plan of campaign, plotted before the agreement, was revealed on March 27th 1998 when a document by its new director of information was leaked to the DUP. It proposed to target non-voters, first-time voters and women, using polls and focus groups, and advocated the selective publication of findings. The proposal to enlist non-political public figures – naming the Church of Ireland primate, Archbishop Robin

Eames – proved damaging (the secretary of state had to apologise to the archbishop). It was clear that the NIO was a player and not a referee.

The campaign polls, including two exit polls on May 22nd, are set out below:

Date	Commissioning body	Polling company
16 April	Guardian/ Irish Times	ICM/MRNI
19 April	Sunday Independent	IMS/UMS
28 April	RTE	Lansdowne/UMS
8 May	NIO	UMS
14 May	NIO	UMS
15 May	Irish Times	ICM/ MRNI
16 May	Irish News/ News Letter	UMS
18 May	Daily Telegraph	Gallup/ MRC
19 May	Belfast Telegraph	UTV/ MRNI
20 May	Irish Independent	IMS/ UMS
21 May	Irish Times	ICM/ MRNI
22 May	The Sunday Times	Coopers and Lybrand
22 May	RTE	UMS

The polls quickly established that the 'yes' camp was ahead and it remained so. The 'no' poll varied and the undecided frequently exceeded 30 per cent. The exit polls revealed that only 52 per cent of voters had made up their mind as soon as the agreement was announced and 24 per cent did so in the last week. The NIO launched a campaign on May 8th to encourage participation. Fewer than 19 per cent did not vote – 200,000 more electors turning out than in the 1997 general election.

The 'no' campaign

◼ **T**he DUP and UK Unionist Party had campaigned against the talks since leaving them in July 1997, in anticipation of an SF presence. They organised rallies across Northern Ireland during the autumn and winter, but their biggest scoop was the acquisition of the NIO strategy document. Their adverts, which parodied the government's 'Its Your Choice' series, were considered so effective by the NIO as to require the threat of legal action.

The day after the agreement was secured, the DUP leader, Rev Ian Paisley, put himself at the head of the 'no' campaign. Its criticism of prisoner releases, the absence of decommissioning, paramilitaries in government and plans for a commission on policing tapped moral concerns about aspects of the agreement; hence the campaign slogan, launched on May 5th – 'It's Right to say No'. The narrow campaign focus and the fact that it had been in action for seven months meant it set the agenda in the early days. 'Have a Heart' stickers and badgers focused attention on the victims of the 'troubles' and helped finance the campaign.

An Ulster Hall rally in Belfast on April 23rd highlighted the divisions in the UUP. The presence of three of the party's ten MPs – William Thompson, Roy Beggs and William Ross – alongside Mr Paisley and Peter Robinson (DUP) and Robert McCartney (UKUP) brought the promise of support from a further three. Despite the fact that 'no' unionists came from several parties – DUP, UKUP, United Unionist and UUP – they shared campaign offices, their activities were focused and they complemented one another. On May 18th the former leader of the Ulster Unionists, Lord Molyneaux, announced he would be voting no.

The independent 'yes' campaign

◼ **T**he 'yes' campaign was launched on April 27th but it had its genesis in a meeting on March 17th and the setting up of a company the next day. It utilised contacts with experience of the Scottish referendum and in the British Labour party with knowledge of 'floating voters'. It aimed its campaign at the 'middle class, middle of the road unionist, women and new voters'; this was similar to the NIO campaign and this worried the organisers, especially after the NIO document was leaked.

The 'yes' campaign planned on a budget of £250,000, raised some £400,000 and spent just over £300,000. It hoped for a unified campaign by all the pro-agreement parties but settled for generating a politically complementary presence. It commissioned research on undecided unionists and sent out 14,000 five-minute videos to first-time voters. It admitted that agenda-setting was difficult with so many diverse campaign groups. But it claimed some success for its breakfasts at the Europa Hotel, and its engagement of the churches, sports stars and the social partners. It also claimed success for its billboards, launched by the former NIO minister Richard Needham on May 5th, and other advertising stunts.

The party 'yes' campaigns

■ **O**ptimistic sentiments about the new politics of pro- versus anti-agreement parties were tested almost to destruction. The pro- parties – UUP, SDLP, SF, Alliance, PUP, UDP and NIWC – did not agree a unified campaign. They also refused the offer from the non-party 'yes' campaign to co-ordinate one for them. The result was a series of separate launches and the spotlight was on the differences in the UUP, the main pro-agreement unionist party.

The Ulster Unionist Council backed the party leader, David Trimble, on the agreement but six of the ten MPs were against and the Orange Order said no even after a meeting with the prime minister. Prisoner releases and decommissioning were the main points of concern and Tony Blair visited three times in May to offer reassurance. On the first trip, he was accompanied by his Conservative predecessor, John Major, and he announced a fund for victims. On the second, the chancellor, Gordon Brown, announced a 'peace through prosperity' investment package of £350 million. And on the third, two days before polling day, Mr Blair issued five handwritten pledges to anxious unionists.

Opinion had begun to move in the 'yes' direction during the final week of campaigning, and the image of the SDLP leader, John Hume, and Mr Trimble on stage with Bono at a U2 concert was taken as a symbol of the new politics. President Clinton, at the G7 summit in Birmingham, said the agreement safeguarded the principle of consent, that everyone would gain from its endorsement and that it would facilitate investment.

There was less uncertainty about the attitude of nationalists to the agreement, which the SDLP regarded as very close to its own prescription. At a special SF ard fheis on May 10th in Dublin, attended by leading IRA prisoners from the Maze and Portlaoise, 331 out of 350 delegates voted to take seats in the new assembly, reversing a policy of 77 years. The reception given to the prisoners, especially the Balcombe Street gang, however had a negative effect on undecided unionists (as did the appearance of the loyalist prisoner Michael Stone at a UDP rally in the Ulster Hall).

The results

■ **O**n polling day, May 22nd, the question was direct: 'Do you support the agreement reached at the multi-party talks on Northern Ireland and set out in Command Paper 3883?' The count took place at a single centre in Belfast the following day, in the presence of the world's media. The turnout of 81.1 per cent was the highest of any election in Northern since the 89 per cent of 1921. The result was:

| Yes | 676,966 | 71.12% |
| No | 274,879 | 28.88% |

The leaders of the DUP and the UKUP left the hall to chants of 'Dinosaur, Dinosaur, Dinosaur ...' from the loyalist parties anticipating the 'new politics'.

The result was decisively in favour of the agreement. One exit poll showed a majority against only in Mr Paisley's North Antrim constituency. There was debate on whether a majority of unionists had voted for the agreement: the two exit polls variously estimated that 55 per cent and 51 per cent of Protestants had voted 'yes'. The 'no' vote was almost exclusively Protestant. In a future system of government based on consensus – not majorities – it was clear the 'no' vote remained a problem.

The assembly election

■ There was no break between the referendum and the assembly election campaigns. The legislation for the elections, the Northern Ireland (Elections) Bill, was subjected to guillotine, so it passed all Commons stages on April 22nd and the Lords on May 6th and 7th. The detailed regulations were contained in an order adapting the Representation of the People Acts to the requirements of PR-STV.

Nominations opened on June 1st, attracting an unprecedented 304 candidates for the 108 seats. There were 17 identifiable party labels and three groups of independents. There was a wide choice in each constituency – 15 candidates on average. The main question was whether the parties could mobilise electors to the same extent as in the referendum. Parties adopted a number of tactics dependent on media collaboration. Most used press conferences to introduce their candidates to the public.

The focus ought to have been the party manifestos, since there was a prospect of responsible party politics for the first time in a generation. Parties proposed a variety of policies, usually arranged in the proposed devolved subject areas. Despite the thinking indicated, the main issues – education, health and the economy and taxation – reflected UK-wide concerns.

But the focus was rather on whether the pro-agreement parties would do well or whether 'no' parties could undermine the settlement. The campaign among the six unionist parties and groups was like a re-run of the referendum. The DUP nominated 34 candidates to fight all 18 constituencies and the UKUP nominated 13 in 12 constituencies, mainly in the east. Their campaign benefited from the division in the UUP.

The loose democratic organisation of the UUP required the leadership to accept that candidate selection was a matter for the constituency associations. Out of 48 UUP candidates officially nominated, six were firm or soft 'no', and five 'no' candidates stood against the official party choices. This opposition to the UUP leadership in 11 of the 18 constituencies was reminiscent of 1973 (and even 1969).

The loyalist parties, represented by the PUP and UDP, were also in competition for unionist votes. The PUP promoted 12 candidates in 11 constituencies, of which only two were in the west. The UDP nominated nine candidates in nine constituencies, with only one in the west. Hence there was enormous competition for unionist votes, especially in the east, running the risk of 'vote shredding'.

The overwhelming support for the agreement among nationalists did not dampen the competition between the SDLP and SF, on grounds of party rivalry. SF again proposed an electoral pact with the SDLP but this was rejected as unncessary under the single transferable vote. The SDLP nominated 38 candidates to fight all 18 constituencies; SF nominated 37, omitting only North Down. In the west and border constituencies SF matched or exceeded the number of SDLP candidates.

The Alliance party dominated the centrist parties, with 22 candidates and a presence in every constituency. There was competition from the Northern Ireland Women's Coalition, with eight candidates. Two fringe parties, the Northern Ireland Conservatives and the Workers' Party, tried to launch a comeback. There was also a range of Labour candidates and two Socialist party candidates. Finally, the Natural Law Party had a presence in each of the 18 constituencies and there was also a range of independents.

Polling day produced a turnout of 68.76 per cent, 4.3 per cent better than for the 1982 assembly but lower than the 70.6 per cent of 1973. The pro-agreement parties polled 75 per cent of the vote, an improvement on the 71 per cent of the referendum. The 'no' parties gained only 28 of the 108 seats, short of a majority of unionists.

Mr Trimble's fear of 'vote shredding' was realised. For the first time in an assembly-type election, the UUP was knocked off top position by the SDLP, with 21.3 per cent as against 22 per cent of first-preference votes. The UUP vote share was down 2.9 per cent on the 1996 forum result and 11.4 per cent since Westminster 1997. The DUP also declined by 0.7 per cent from 1996 but its partner UKUP increased its share by 0.8 per cent. Even the small loyalist parties, the PUP and UDP, found their vote shrinking by around 1 per cent each. The only other group of unionists to gain was the independents opposed to the agreement. The UUP candidates opposed to the agreement performed worse than those who stood as independent or United Unionist candidates.

The nationalist and republican parties again polled well. While the SDLP topped the poll for the first time, its share at 22 per cent was only 0.6 per cent better than in 1996. SF, however, experienced its fifth increase since 1993 and with 17.6 per cent, 2.1 per cent higher than 1996, it further narrowed the gap with the SDLP. In 1992 the nationalist vote had split 70:30 in favour of the SDLP but in 1998 the ratio was 55:45.

In the allocation of seats, however, the UUP came out as the largest party with 28, followed by the SDLP with 24. The 20 DUP, 5 UKUP and three Independent Unionists totalled 28 – the same number as the UU – but the two PUP members brought the pro-agreement unionist total to 30. Together with the 24 SDLP, 18 SF, six Alliance and two Women's Coalition, some 80 members were pro-agreement. But several elected UUP members were known to have doubts. One of the moments of the television coverage of the election was the clash (Belfast Telegraph, June 27th 1998) between two UUP MPs, Ken Maginnis (pro) and Jeffrey Donaldson (anti). When the former claimed his colleague was gloating over party difficulties, the latter claimed that Mr Maginnis, the director of elections, 'should hold his head in shame … He has presided over one of the worst electoral disasters for the UUP in recent years.'

There had been some discussion soon after the referendum about a new pro- and anti- political cleavage. Indeed, Séamus Mallon (SDLP) had said that voting for other pro-agreement parties, including unionists, had to be considered. And the key requirement of the new settlement was co-operation between the SDLP and the UUP. But the RTE/UMS exit poll revealed that only 1 per cent of SDLP voters had given a second preference to another party and only 4 per cent a third preference; for UUP voters the figures were 1 and 3 per cent respectively. Indeed the transfers indicated possibly the most communal voting pattern since the reintroduction of PR-STV in 1973.

1998 Assembly election results

Party	1st preferences	% votes	Seats
SDLP	177,963	22.0	24
UUP	172,225	21.3	28
DUP	146,989	18.1	20
SF	142,858	17.6	18
AP	52,636	6.5	6
UKUP	36,541	4.5	5
Ind U	23,127	2.9	3
PUP	20,634	2.6	2
NIWC	13,019	1.6	2
UDP	8,651	1.1	0
Lab	2,729	0.3	0
WP	1,989	0.2	0
Con	1,835	0.2	0
UIM	1,212	0.1	0
NLP	832	0.1	0
SP	789	0.1	0
GP	710	0.1	0
Ind N	528	0.1	0
Ind LAB	121	0.0	0
Energy	15	0.0	0
Ind	4,914	0.6	0
Total	810,317	100.0	108

16

The decommissioning issue

Paul Bew

■ **T**he decommissioning issue first raised its – for some – ugly head on October 9th 1993. Speaking on RTE, Sir Patrick Mayhew, the then Northern Ireland secretary, said the IRA would have to make its guns and explosives 'available' to show that violence was over.

The context is clear. There were widespread rumours of secret British government-IRA contacts; these were to be definitively exposed in the Observer on November 28th. In such an atmosphere of nervousness – with widespread unionist fear of 'betrayal' – Sir Patrick felt it necessary to offer this reassurance.

It worked at the time: the then UUP leader, James Molyneaux, was surprisingly relaxed about the revelation of the secret contacts. Nor was decommissioning simply a British government political position; it also represented the profound conviction of the government in Dublin. Both felt that it was wrong to negotiate with paramilitary groups who still retained a threat of violence. Only Ian Paisley predicted correctly that this would happen in the end.

December 15th 1993 was a solemn day, the day of the Downing Street Declaration, which spoke of the need for a 'permanent' renunciation of violence. Offering a gloss on the meaning of the reference, the republic's foreign affairs minister, Dick Spring, told the Dáil: 'Questions were asked on how to determine a permanent cessation of violence. We are talking about the handing up of arms and are insisting that it would not be simply a temporary cessation of violence to see what the political process offers. There can be no equivocation in relation to the determination of both governments in that regard.' The point was later reiterated by Sir Patrick: 'If they hold on to arms, if you know they have got them, then quite patently they are not giving them up for good.'

Being a highly capable leader, the SF president, Gerry Adams, was, of course, quite aware of the position of the two governments. On January 8th 1994, in an Irish News interview, Mr Adams criticised the British government: 'Mr Mayhew goes on to say "Well the exploratory dialogue will be so we can discuss with Sinn Féin how the IRA will hand over their weapons." So I say to myself: "This is what they want. They want the IRA to stop so that Sinn Féin can have the privilege twelve years later, having been properly sanitised and come out of quarantine, to have discussions with senior civil servants on how the IRA can hand over their weapons." I hear that reiterated again and again by Douglas Hurd, by John Major, by Patrick Mayhew.' At the party's ard fheis in west Dublin, Mr Adams said to loud applause: 'Does anyone really expect the IRA to cease its activities so that British civil servants can discuss with Sinn Féin the surrender of IRA weapons after we have been "decontaminated"?'

This did not stop Mr Adams telling the Irish Times on June 14th 1995: 'The demand for the surrender of IRA weapons as a precondition to negotiations was never mentioned before 31 August [1994] ... In my view had a surrender of IRA weapons been imposed as a precondition to peace negotiations prior to the ceasefire, it is possible there would have been no IRA cessation on 1 September last year.' This was a spectacular case of amnesia, but it has to be said that it was collective.

As early as late 1994, and certainly by 1995, nationalist Ireland, north and south, decided the arms issue was a distraction. Those who talked nervously of the 'politics of threat' were acting in bad faith. The IRA cease-fire was a splendid offer and political talks should begin rapidly. It was Perfidious Albion backed by reactionary unionist intransigence which was destroying everything and provoking the IRA to break its cease-fire, as happened at Canary Wharf in February 1996. It was asserted again and again – quite falsely – that the decommissioning pre-condition had only been introduced after the IRA cease-fire of August 1994.

Decommissioning has been an enormously difficult issue to deal with in the process – in part because it was not, for a long time, amenable to the political fudge which has otherwise worked so well. It is, therefore, perhaps understandable that the entire nationalist bloc went into denial about the complex history of the issue and the evidence which had been first brought to it by its own newspaper in the north.

Such was the scale of feeling on the matter that even skilful diplomats could apparently deceive themselves. At one celebrated Anglo-Irish liaison committee of top officials, the representatives of London handed over to those from Dublin a list of statements on the matter from the latter quarter – starring, of course, that by the foreign affairs minister. The Irish delegation, which may well have included the authors of that statement, lapsed into uncharacteristic silence. Later, out of office, the taoiseach at the time, Albert Reynolds, was, in effect, to write that Mr Spring had been acting on his own; no one at the time had suggested anything of the sort.

Decommissioning prevented an agreement under the Major government. The Blair government, backed by a large majority, made an immediate decision to downplay it in favour of the 'consent principle' – the oft-rehearsed reassurance to unionists that there can be no change in the constitutional status of Northern Ireland without majority endorsement. This approach paid dividends, in the sense that it permitted the negotiation of the Belfast Agreement. But the decommissioning issue would not go away. It delayed the formation of the Executive Committee until December 1999; it led to the suspension in February 2000; after further negotiation, a temporary resolution allowed the executive to be re-established in May.

That 'resolution' has been characterised, at last, by the discovery of ways to describe the issue which allow both sides to claim victory, or at any rate avoid humiliating defeat. This is the core characteristic of the process; nor is it an entirely cosmetic one, 'just for the optics'.

Unionists in 1995 refused the Framework Document's 'cross-borderism', but with the removal of concepts like 'dynamic' and 'harmonising' they signed up for meaningful north-south co-operation in 1998. Important safeguards were won, but at the same time the unionist political class did move. Nor have republicans handed over a bullet – as their slogan warned they wouldn't. But the confidence-building measure of international inspection of arms dumps does rather precisely meet Sir Patrick's original request in October 1993, that the IRA make its guns and explosives available to show that violence is over.

17

The Programme for Government

Robin Wilson

Institutionitis

■ **A**n unfortunate effect of the process of elaboration of the Belfast Agreement was a narrowly institutional focus. In the absence of constitutional consensus, all attention was displaced on to the construction of an institutional matrix which spatchcocked together otherwise competing constitutional propositions. Some incoherence inevitably resulted – arguably, the idea of forming the Executive Committee using the d'Hondt rule, for example (see chapter 8).

But the major difficulty was the near absence of any pre-agreement debate on policy objectives; rather than form following function, the institutional architecture was worked out quite in abstraction from what the new institutions would be for. The only significant exception was the equality provisions, which essentially carried forward the direct-rule administration's proposals in the white paper Partnership for Equality (Cm 3890) published a few weeks earlier.

This process continued after the agreement, notably in the way the departmental configuration was governed by the politically-driven requirement of 10 ministries, despite the fragmentation effect on government.

This problem was not confined to Northern Ireland. Even in Scotland, where a consensus around the idea of Scottish autonomy – if not its extent – was relatively settled, 'the debate around the Parliament centred primarily on institutional concerns'. As a result, 'The establishment of a Scottish Parliament in May 1999 has yet to show much in the way of energy and vision and has certainly failed to capture the political imagination' (Hassan and Warhurst, 1999: 6, 8).

The policy deficit

■ **D**irect rule has not survived for all but a few months of the last 28 years out of any appetite at Westminster for direct involvement in the government of Northern Ireland over that period – quite the contrary. But within the region itself the effect of the unbending of the springs of political action from 1972 onwards only gradually became apparent as direct rule became prolonged. The Opsahl report, two decades on, diagnosed its 'debilitating' impact: 'political parties are poorly organised in terms of political development and policy-making'. As one witness to the commission put it, 'We are keeping our politicians in kindergarten' (Pollak, 1993: 15, 14).

There were three major disincentives to policy elaboration by the parties under direct rule. The first was a lack of interest: a worthy document on (say) health policy would hardly secure a mention in regional media obsessed with the narrow agenda of constitutional politics and security. The second was a lack of consequences: the chances of a policy proposal being accepted by the direct-rule administration depended on its prior consonance with the ideological stance of the party in power at Westminster. And the third was a lack of necessity: the electoral success or failure of the parties bore no correlation to the thinness or otherwise of their policy portfolios, and Northern Ireland could be governed on an auto-pilot basis where central-government policies were adopted wholesale with minor tweaking by Stormont officials.

Perhaps most serious was the way direct rule separated the articulation of policy preferences by regionally elected representatives from responsibility for their execution. For the politicians, this was experienced as an immensely frustrating lack of accountability. But it also stimulated an oppositionalist culture, where the opportunity costs of particular preferences did not have to be addressed. Hence, for example, the tendency of regional politicians to defend the retention of all services at any acute hospitals in their constituency, whatever the consequences for the rationalisation of the acute-hospital matrix necessary to ensure adequate standards of care for patients as a whole (Wilford and Wilson, 2000).

This problem was thus particularly acute in the absence of any serious debate until very recently about priority-setting in public expenditure (Wilson, 1999). Northern Ireland has enjoyed relatively favourable public-expenditure treatment under direct rule, through a combination of the operation of the Barnett formula, special programmes and a general flexibility owing to the security situation and the small size of the numbers from a Treasury perspective. This soft-budget environment favoured demands to throw money at any problem that emerged, rather than eliciting an innovative policy response.

It represents a major cultural shift for regional politicians to face up to the 'hard choices' control of most of the Northern Ireland block implies. The announcement by the finance minister Mark Durkan (SDLP) of the first "home grown" draft budget in October 2000 was thus an important positive development. And the fiscal relaxation by the 'iron chancellor', Gordon Brown, in the second Comprehensive Spending Review will ease the pressures. But spending allocations retain the potential to cause tension around the executive table.

Gluing government together

■ **C**onversely, agreement on the Programme for Government presented a critical symbolic opportunity to express the cohesion of the new administration. In the absence of common party allegiance, the programme can provide 'glue' to hold the Executive Committee together, setting the wider context in which departmental agenda, in tandem, have to be pursued. In more disciplinary mode, it gives the first and deputy first minister the 'whip' to ensure other ministers stay on a common path. And its preparation, and subsequent annual review, offer a crucial focus for wider democratic involvement, in the Northern Ireland Assembly and beyond, in the debate about the future shape of the region.

As material changes visible to the public at large will not be substantial in the short term, tangible improvements in the conduct of politics can nevertheless sustain confidence in the project. In particular, the electorate will be watchful for evidence of collaborative behaviour between the parties to the Executive Committee, and especially between the first and deputy first minister. Moreover, changes in style can in themselves improve performance – rendering the whole Executive Committee greater than the sum of its parts through the accumulation of trust and mutual confidence. If key actors in civil society feel they are engaged by the new politics, they can be expected in turn to help deliver policy initiatives in which the agencies of government may only have a brokering or enabling role.

In October 2000, the Executive Committee published a draft programme for consultation with Assembly committees and the public.

'Joined-up' government

■ **A** key task of the programme is to weld government together in an administrative, as well as political, sense. After all, governments policy initiatives fall. Yet citizens do not experience their problems in neat departmental boxes. Most difficult for government are the 'wicked' issues which are a product of a range of factors and which therefore particularly require 'joined-up' solutions.

Two issues which are particularly wicked in Northern Ireland are sectarianism and social exclusion. In many ways what defines – and scars – the region to an observer are:

(a) its division at all levels along strict sectarian lines, with the evacuation of any sense of a civic society or of a wider cosmopolitan world; and

(b) the ghettoisation of its unskilled working class and lumpenproletariat (celebrated in a compensatory but wholly imaginary way by paramilitary figures in such 'communities').

Clearly, neither of these problems could be resolved overnight. But, while recognising the constraints on its power and resources, a devolved administration would surely need to make an impact in these crucial areas, if it was to be able credibly to claim that it was making a difference.

Not only does the Programme for Government have the capacity to cement relationships between the parties within Northern Ireland, and so to attenuate the debilitating nationalist-unionist tension (which itself should improve governance by enhancing trust). Similarly, on the all-Ireland national level, north-south co-ordination and joint implementation have the capacity to undermine enemy-images and end what the first minister, Mr Trimble, has referred to as the 'cold war' between the two parts of the island. It is now widely accepted, in the era of the Celtic Tiger, that there are considerable north-south synergies to be secured through policy co-ordination.

Even if the first draft programme is rather modest and aspirational, many of these themes are reflected in it (Northern Ireland Executive, 2000).

Can the centre hold?

■ **T**he Programme for Government is of great significance to political stability in Northern Ireland. It has the potential to build virtuous circles of trust, both across the sectarian divide and between rulers and ruled, which can begin to undo decades of vicious circles of polarisation. It just might, in a word, allow Northern Ireland to be normal.

Bibliography

Hassan, G and Warhurst, C (1999), 'Tomorrow's Scotland', in Hassan and Warhurst eds, A Different Future: A Moderniser's Guide to Scotland, Edinburgh/Glasgow: Centre for Scottish Public Policy / The Big Issue in Scotland

Northern Ireland Executive (2000), Draft Programme for Government, Belfast

Pollak, A (ed) (1993), A Citisens' Inquiry: The Opsahl Report on Northern Ireland, Dublin: Lilliput

Wilford, R and Wilson, R (2000), 'Northern Ireland', in Jervis, P and Plowden, W (eds), Devolution and Health: First Annual Report of a Project to Monitor the Impact of Devolution on the United Kingdom's Health Services, London: Constitution Unit

Wilson, R (ed) (1999), Hard Choices: Policy Autonomy and Priority-setting in Public Expenditure, Belfast: Democratic Dialogue / Eastern Health and Social Services Board / Northern Ireland Economic Council

18

Financial arrangements
Richard Barnett

Introduction

■ In making his first budget statement to the assembly, Mark Durkan, minister of finance and personnel, said (Northern Ireland Assembly Report, 1999): 'The management of public spending is one of the fundamental responsibilities of any government, and this is the first time in almost 30 years that local politicians have had the privilege to accept this responsibility.' And he went on: 'We now have to move on from championing a few issues to deciding priorities among all of the issues – from opposing to leading – and hence earning the respect of those who entrusted us with this role. We must graduate from making demands to making decisions.'

In the context of the government of Northern Ireland, the management of public expenditure will, however, entail a more limited exercise than is generally the case. For most governments such an exercise involves three inter-related policy decisions:

- determination of the total size of the public budget,
- allocation of the budget between policy areas, and
- funding of the budget through tax and public borrowing.

To a very large extent, the financial arrangements under which the government of Northern Ireland operates will mean that budgetary politics will only be concerned with the second of these. Government will be operating in the context of a zero-sum budgetary politics – making decisions about how a fixed budget is allocated between competing policy priorities.

Financial arrangements

■ The government has two sources of funding for the services for which it is responsible:

- a block grant from, and determined in size by, the central government at Westminster; and
- he proceeds of the regional rate.

The block grant is by far the larger of these and, given reasonable (and politically acceptable) levels of the regional rate, will continue to be so. To all intents and purposes the government will thus operate within a fixed-budget constraint.

The size of the block grant is determined by the application of the Barnett formula. Joel (now Lord) Barnett was chief secretary to the Treasury in the Labour government of 1974-79, when the formula was introduced to determine the budgetary allocations to the territorial departments in Northern Ireland, Scotland and Wales. Essentially, it is population-based and applies to changes in the level of public expenditure.

During the periodic spending reviews, changes in public expenditure for the Westminster-based departments are agreed. Then, in the case of devolved services, the Northern Ireland block grant is changed in line with movements in comparable programmes in Great Britain, by applying a percentage weighting (currently 2.91) representing the population ratio between Northern Ireland and the rest of the UK. Thus, if expenditure on education in Britain is increased by £100 million, £2.91 million is added to the region's block grant. While the overall change in the block grant is built up by aggregating changes in individual Westminster programmes – education, health and so on – the Northern Ireland government nevertheless remains free to allocate monies from the block grant as it sees fit.

As already noted, the formula applies only to changes in public expenditure. The level is determined by that prevailing when the formula was introduced plus its subsequent applications. As the then prime minister, Lord (Jim) Callaghan, noted during the debate on the Government of Wales Bill in the Lords, the formula added 'something which was fairly rational onto something which was completely irrational' (Bogdanor, 1999). That is, there has been no assessment as to whether the inherited base of the formula represents spending needs.

Northern Ireland has enjoyed a relatively high level of *per capita* public expenditure, but as a result application of the formula means that percentage increases in public expenditure in Northern Ireland will be less than those in Great Britain. This was anticipated when the formula was introduced and convergence in *per capita* expenditure between the different parts of the UK was seen to be a desirable feature. It does mean, of course, that through time the government of Northern Ireland will receive a smaller percentage share of overall UK public expenditure. It will be conducting zero-sum budgetary politics in the context of an overall budget which is falling relative to that for the UK as a whole.

The regional rate is unique to Northern Ireland and is a consequence of the limited role local government plays in the region.

It applies to both domestic and non-domestic property and is set by the Stormont government. Essentially, it was introduced to compensate for the fact that within Northern Ireland the regional government provides services – such as primary and secondary education – which elsewhere in the UK are provided by local government and funded (in part, at least) through local taxation. The revenue raised by the regional rate is not, however, assigned to specific services and is added to the block grant to give the total budget available for government expenditure.[1]

Budgetary accountability

■ **A**s Bognador (1999) and Heald (1998) have noted, the Barnett formula was introduced to allocate funds within government – between Westminster central departments – and is now being used to distribute funds between different levels of government: the central government and the devolved administrations in Northern Ireland, Scotland and Wales. While there may be some concerns about its suitability for the former (Barnett and Hutchinson, 1998), more fundamental issues arise concerning its suitability for the latter.

Before devolution regional decision-makers (the secretaries of state and their ministerial teams) had discretion to vary policy but they always had overarching policy objectives, in line with the UK government of which they were members. With devolution this congruence is likely to cease. Indeed, one of the prime objectives of devolution is to enable regional preferences to be reflected in policy decisions. A possible consequence is that regional government will seek to blame central government when it fails to provide any services to the standard desired by the electorate. As Bloomfield and Carter (1998: 5) warn, regional government may 'spend its time complaining about the parsimony of the (Westminster) Treasury'.

This may especially be the case in Northern Ireland where, as noted above, application of the Barnett formula will lead to a relatively smaller budget from which to fund services. Financial arrangements which rely principally on a block grant by application of the formula will lead to a blurring of budgetary accountability.

Budgetary accountability requires that there is a match at the margin between expenditure and taxation (or more generally funding) responsibility. There is no such match in the fiscal arrangements under which the government of Northern Ireland will operate. As noted, the only tax under its control is the regional rate, and this is not a tax which budgetary theory would suggest should be used to bring about accountability (Barnett and Knox, 1992). Such a tax should be one borne by the majority of the electorate and clearly linked to spending decisions at Stormont. A regional income tax would fit the bill.

It is unlikely, of course, that any politician will push for the introduction of a tax. Yet without it accountability will be blurred and tensions are likely to arise between central and regional government.

The future

■ The Barnett formula has proved a remarkably robust mechanism for allocating funds within government. Its sustainability as a means of allocating resources between governments must, however, be open to question. In addition to the accountability problem, there is the fact that the formula is purely population-based. Given the relatively high historic base to which it is applied, this has not raised serious issues. Through time, though, its internal mechanics will push towards convergence in the level of *per capita* public expenditure in the various parts of the UK. As it does so, issues will arise about differential expenditure needs – the number in need of medical treatment, the number of school children, the number of elderly people and so on – and the differential costs of providing services in predominantly rural areas such as Northern Ireland. But these are likely to be for the medium to longer term.

In the immediate future, the government will be embarking on the form of budgetary politics outlined by Mr Durkan in his first budget statement. Given the timing of devolution to Northern Ireland, the new government's first budget was a roll-forward of the inherited expenditure plans. The real hard choices began with the first domestically crafted draft budget of October 2000. They were made easier by the chancellor's announcement in July 2000 on the Comprehensive Spending Review which, via application of the Barnett formula, will lead to an increase in the Northern Ireland block grant.

But relative to what is happening in England – and the electorate will make comparisons – increases in some areas will only be achieved by reductions in others. Also, some ministers, notably those from the SDLP and SF, are likely to look to policy in the republic as a guide to what they might seek to implement in the north. Given the current allocation of ministerial portfolios, such an influence may be brought to bear in the policy areas which dominate the budget: education and health. This influence is likely to lead to greater tension in the immediate future, and will add an interesting dimension to budgetary politics in Northern Ireland.

Bibliography

Barnett, R and Hutchinson, G (1998), 'Public expenditure on the eve of devolution', in Hard Choices: Policy Autonomy and Priority-setting in Public Expenditure, Belfast: Democratic Dialogue / Northern Ireland Economic Council / Eastern Health and Social Services Board, 48-70

Barnett, R and Knox, C (1992), 'Accountability and local budgetary policy: unitary principles', Policy and Politics, 20: 265-276

Bloomfield, K and Carter, C (1998), 'Introduction', in People and Government: Questions for Northern Ireland, Belfast: Chief Executives' Forum / Joseph Rowntree Foundation

Bognador, V (1999), Devolution in the United Kingdom, Oxford: Oxford University Press

Heald, D (1998), 'Fiscal opportunities', in Hard Choices: Policy Autonomy and Priority-setting in Public Expenditure, Belfast: Democratic Dialogue / Northern Ireland Economic Council / Eastern Health and Social Services Board, 71-87

Notes to the text

[1] In the immediate future, the government will also receive some monies from the European Union which are additional to the block grant from Westminster.

19

A civil service and a civil society
Colin Knox

Introduction

■ **P**ublic services in Northern Ireland operate through a complex arrangement of central government departments, agencies, boards, trusts, non-departmental public bodies and district councils. The system is a product of the political turmoil from the late 60s onwards and its consequences for the machinery of government. While the abuse of powers in service delivery by former public bodies (particularly local authorities) played a major part in the creation of the present system of administration, this was compounded by government policies in Great Britain, adopted in the region, which eroded local democracy and contributed to the growth of quangos and other non-elected public bodies.

The priority accorded to constitutional, political and security matters allowed public policy to rest with unelected civil servants or politicians who had no electoral constituency in Northern Ireland.

Essential public services, such as health, education and housing, operated under the aegis of appointed boards and the major repository of power was the Northern Ireland secretary. Throughout 'direct rule', citizens of Northern Ireland acquiesced in a system of public services euphemistically described as having a 'democratic deficit' or being in a state of 'permanent impermanence' (Bloomfield and Carter, 1998).

The civil service

■ **W**ith government devolved in December 1999 and, after the February suspension, once more in May 2000, the functions of the six central government departments in Northern Ireland were reorganised amongst 10 new departments, and the Office of the First and Deputy First Minister, under the direct control of ministers from the region. The secretary of state retains responsibility for excepted and reserved matters – such as police, security policy, prisons, criminal justice and taxation – through the Northern Ireland Office. The larger number, disproportionate size and clustering of functions in the new departments had little basis in administrative logic but was the product of political negotiations arising from the agreement.

The new devolved tier has added to both administrative complexity and representational overload in the region. With a population of 1.67 million, Northern Ireland now enjoys three MEPs, 18 MPs, 108 members of the legislative assembly (MLAs) and 582 district councillors. Without tax-raising powers there is a natural concern about the increasing cost of administering public services.

This was recognised by the first minister and deputy first minister in their proposals for new departmental structures (New Northern Ireland Assembly Report 7, February 15th 1999): 'We recognise that the increasing number of departments inevitably involves some dislocation and diseconomies. We share the firm view expressed during our consultations with parties that the additional costs should be offset by rationalising the remainder of public administration in Northern Ireland.' This has inevitably resulted in speculation about the future configuration of sub-regional government: local government, quangos and the relationship between the assembly and the vibrant civil society which has burgeoned in Northern Ireland.

Local government

■ Local government was perhaps the greatest casualty of direct-rule arrangements. Councils' record of discrimination in appointments, gerrymandering and unfair methods of housing allocation played a large part in the civil strife of the late 60s. This culminated in a reform process dictated by Westminster, consequent upon the Macrory report of 1970 (Cmnd 546) which created a single tier of 26 district councils to discharge largely prosaic functions.

Since its consequent reform in 1973, local government has played a minor role in public-service provision (Birrell and Hayes, 1999). The councils are limited chiefly to delivery of minor regulatory services. They have three main roles:

- executive, in that they provide certain regulatory services (such as building regulations, environmental health and licensing of dance halls and cinemas) and a limited range of functions (such as street cleaning, refuse collection, cemeteries and crematoria, recreation and tourist amenities and economic development);
- representative, where members are nominated to other bodies (such as area education and library boards); and
- consultative, where councils' views are sought on centrally provided services (such as planning, roads, water and housing).

The emasculation of local government is illustrated by its location within overall public administration. Estimated net spending by councils in 2000-01 amounts to £275 million, out of a Northern Ireland public-expenditure budget of £9.9 billion – about 2.8 per cent. Yet local authorities are important for other reasons.

First, progressive local authorities have played a much wider role than their limited responsibilities would suggest. They have acted at the hub of economic and social development in their areas, as a catalyst for involvement of other public and voluntary agencies and the private sector. Secondly, in the long absence of any devolved arrangements (and until the new assembly takes root), councillors continue to be the most accessible source for constituents with concerns about centrally provided services (housing, planning and social security in particular).

Thirdly, local authorities have become pivotal brokers in partnership arrangements designed to deliver European Union programmes. In 1995, the EU launched the Special Support Programme for Peace and Reconciliation, a 300 million ecu (£215 million) package designed to reinforce progress towards a peaceful and stable society following the cease-fires. District partnerships, representing each council area, and comprising equal numbers of councillors, community/voluntary-sector representatives, and the business, trade union and statutory sectors, approved plans for local activities to advance the objectives of the programme. The process aims to achieve peace and reconciliation by broadening participation through socially inclusive programmes in employment, productive investment and urban/rural regeneration. The district partnership model has been very successful in widening the basis of participation throughout the 26 councils (Hughes, Knox, Murray and Greer, 1998). A follow-on programme, Peace 2 (£276 million), has been approved for 2000-04. It will carry forward the distinctive aspects of the current peace programme but, according to government, with a more economic focus.

Quangos

■ **A**side from the central machinery of government, and to add to its administrative mosaic, Northern Ireland has a large number of quangos (quasi-autonomous non-governmental organisations). Quangos cover a variety of bodies exercising executive, advisory and tribunal functions. In Northern Ireland this includes bodies as diverse as the area education and library boards (five), area health and social services boards (four), the Local Enterprise Development Unit, the Northern Ireland Housing Executive, the Labour Relations Agency and the Northern Ireland Tourist Board. Some of the larger executive quangos undertake functions performed by local authorities in Britain.

The proper and effective operation of quangos is all the more important because of the absence, up until now, of a democratic tier of regional government. Government data for 1998-99 show that there were 46 executive non-departmental public bodies and 32 National Health Service bodies in Northern Ireland with an expenditure of £5.5 billion, or over half the public-sector purse (Department of Finance and Personnel and HM Treasury, 1999). The Cabinet Office publication Public Bodies lists a total of 148 bodies (executive, advisory NDPBs and tribunals) operating in Northern Ireland, accounting for more than 2,000 public appointments.[1]

Concerns have been expressed about both the operation of quangos and the appointment process (Bradley, 1994). Critics tend to focus on the number of quangos, the scope for improvements in their efficiency and financial management, and whether their functions are necessary or could be performed differently; but there are also concerns about the procedures by which board members are appointed. In November 1997 the Labour government issued a consultation paper, Opening Up Quangos, as a UK-wide document for public discussion, but its salience in Northern Ireland was paramount given the problems of accountability and loss of democratic control associated with direct rule. Suggestions for improvement arising from the consultation, appearing in a 1998 paper, Quangos: Opening the Doors, included encouraging non-departmental public bodies to offer greater access to information by publishing annual reports, publicising reports of meetings and, where possible, making meetings more accessible.

It is not surprising that quangos have become the target of criticism. Charges of a quangocrats' clique characterised by a 'don't rock the boat' mentality are levelled at many of these bodies created under direct rule to fill the gap left by the absence of an elected assembly. With government devolved once again their *raison d'être* is being questioned and the assembly sees an opportunity to achieve administrative efficiencies through rationalisation or abolition.

Civil society

■ **T**hroughout direct rule, and in the absence of a stable society, the voluntary/community sector filled the vacuum through capacity-building, community engagement and service delivery. In 1975 some 500 community groups and associations were in existence (Birrell and Murie, 1980), but the Northern Ireland Council for Voluntary Action has estimated the current total of voluntary organisations, community groups and charitable bodies at 5,500. In 1990 one voluntary-sector advocate wrote (Oliver, 1990: 374): 'The non-profit sector, in its broadest sense, is well placed to stake its claim to make a significant contribution to social change and progress in this climate; it operates at all levels (local, regional and central); it combines geographically and sectorally based interests; it draws its constituency from "both sides of the community". If representative of local interests, it has the potential to be the only representative movement to achieve real change.'

The interests of the voluntary sector are wide-ranging and embrace planning, advocacy, service delivery and job creation in a manner complementary to public bodies and the private sector. The vibrant civil society and its active involvement as non-elected participants in the decision-making process have not met universal approval, however, particularly among some assembly members. One Ulster Unionist MLA expressed the view (Birnie, 1999: 8): 'Under the new political dispensation these groups should not be as influential as they were during 1972-99. Elected and representative democracy should not be smothered by some of the rather exotic political developments of the direct rule period.'

But the sector's continued involvement in decision-making is guaranteed through the Civic Forum, which acts as a consultative mechanism for the assembly on social, economic and cultural matters. Of its representatives 18 (out of 60) were selected by NICVA, Disability Action, the Rural Community Network and the Women's Resource and Development Agency.

The future

■ **T**he current system of public administration in Northern Ireland is patently unsatisfactory. Direct rule became an excuse for administrative inertia. The assumption that no changes could be made to public-service delivery in the absence of progress on the constitutional front created and embedded an array of boards, trusts, quangos and civil-service departments characterised by official indifference. The key power brokers were senior civil servants, whose departmental responsibilities went largely unchecked by Westminster politicians consumed by political/constitutional and security matters. A fundamental review is needed of governance arrangements in Northern Ireland.

There is a real need to assess the role of local authorities, the only enduring democratic forum throughout direct rule, yet limited in their responsibilities. This will necessarily include a review of the plethora of government agencies, boards and trusts that provide services undertaken by local government in Britain. This review must include the newly restructured civil-service departments: it would be a nonsense to consider economic development or planning without examining the role and functions of departments working in these areas. Moreover, central-local government relations have, not surprisingly, plummeted over time as a result of civil servants (planners in particular) ignoring council input to decision-making.

An overhaul of the burgeoning quango state is also imperative. It is unacceptable under devolved arrangements to have 50 per cent of public expenditure controlled by non-departmental public bodies in the charge of appointees. While the rationale for establishing such bodies was often to remove their functions from partisan government (fair employment, housing, police), the current devolved institutions (with safeguards) should obviate the need for a large number.

Bibliography

Birnie, E (1999), 'Ulster must prepare for New Political Change', News Letter, December 30th

Birrell, D and Hayes, A (1999), The Local Government System in Northern Ireland, Dublin: Institute of Public Administration

Birrell, D and Murie, A (1980), Policy and Government in Northern Ireland: Lessons of Devolution, Dublin: Gill and Macmillan

Bloomfield, K and Carter, C (eds.) (1998) People and Government: Questions for Northern Ireland, York: Joseph Rowntree Foundation and Chief Executives Forum

Bradley, C (1994), 'Keeping a Secret', Fortnight 335: 25-26

Department of Finance and Personnel and HM Treasury (1999), Northern Ireland Expenditure Plans and Priorities: The Government's Expenditure Plans 1999-2000 to 2001-2002, Belfast: Stationery Office

Hughes, J, Knox, C, Murray, M and Greer, J (1998), Partnership Governance in Northern Ireland: The Path to Peace, Dublin: Oak Tree Press

Oliver, Q (1990), 'Community development in areas of political and social conflict: the case of Northern Ireland', Community Development Journal 25(4): 370-376

Notes to the text

[1] List updated recently (April 2000) by the publication Northern Ireland Non-Departmental Public Bodies 1999, Belfast: Stationery Office